100 HEIRLOOM
TOMATOES
for the
AMERICAN
GARDEN

100 HEIRLOOM TOMATOES *for the* AMERICAN GARDEN

by CAROLYN J. MALE

photographs by FRANK IANNOTTI

foreword by KENT WHEALY

WORKMAN PUBLISHING · NEW YORK

The person most responsible for my continuing interest in and love of heirloom tomatoes is Craig LeHoullier. His infectious enthusiasm, photographic memory for all things tomatoey, and continued support has endured for almost twelve years. The persons who made it possible for me to grow and evaluate over 1,000 varieties of tomatoes are Sue and Charlie Brizzell. Charlie allowed me to transplant at his greenhouses, grew on the plants for me, prepared my field, cultivated, and fertilized for me.

I thank the following for exchange of seeds and/or great tomato talk: Craig LeHoullier, Bill Minkey, Joe Bratka, Ulrike Paradine, Steve Draper, Tad Smith, Calvin Waite, Amy Goldman, Fax Stinnett, Dennis Sherwood, Jeff Dawson, Chuck Wyatt, Dennis Sherwood, Jeff McCormack, Linda Sapp, Glenn Drowns, Rob Johnston, and a score of others too numerous to mention.

Thanks to Andy Smith for spirited chat and general tomato history. The strong support shown by Kent and Diane Whealy and the staff at SSE has been very gratifying. Debra and Wayne Freihofer and Amy Goldman garden near me and are wonderful "tomato" friends. The contribution of Kees Sahin of The Netherlands relative to certain varietal histories and overall knowledge of seeds has been invaluable.

Finally, without John Meils, my editor, to spur me onward with grace, wit, and great skill, this book would not have matured. Mary Wilkinson did a Brobdingnagian job of copyediting, and artfully brought this book to fruition. And Frank Iannotti's photographs are magnificent.

LIBRARY OF CONGRESS CATALOGING-IN-PUBLICATION DATA

MALE, CAROLYN J.

100 HEIRLOOM TOMATOES FOR THE AMERICAN GARDEN

BY CAROLYN J. MALE;

PHOTOGRAPHS BY FRANK IANNOTTI.

P.   CM.

ISBN-13: 978-0-7611-1400-0

1. TOMATOES--HEIRLOOM VARIETIES. I. TITLE. II. TITLE: ONE
HUNDRED HEIRLOOM TOMATOES FOR THE AMERICAN GARDEN.

SB349.M356   1999

635' .6427--dc21   99-17665   CIP

WORKMAN PUBLISHING COMPANY, INC.

225 VARICK STREET

NEW YORK, NY 10014-4381

MANUFACTURED IN CHINA

FIRST PRINTING MAY 1999

10 9 8 7 6 5 4 3 2

CONTENTS

APPENDIXES

Foreword

Today's gardeners, often disappointed and dissatisfied with the varieties of tomatoes commercially available, are collecting and distributing heirloom tomatoes from every corner of the world. Nearly 1,000 members of the Seed Savers Exchange (SSE) used the Seed Savers 1999 Yearbook to offer 21,500 listings of rare vegetables and fruits— and nearly one-third of those listings were tomatoes. In the Preservation Gardens at Heritage Farm (SSE's headquarters near Decorah, Iowa), vast collections of 18,000 rare vegetables are being maintained, including 4,500 tomatoes. The tomato diversity available to today's gardeners is absolutely dazzling.

During SSE's quarter-century of growth, no member has done more to popularize heirloom tomatoes and increase the diversity of available offerings than Dr. Carolyn Male. Carolyn has been an extremely active member of SSE for a decade, and a Lifetime Member since 1994. During those years she has offered hundreds of heirloom tomatoes to other members of SSE (up to 230 varieties per year), reuniting many gardeners with the heirlooms of their childhood. She has trialed heirloom tomatoes for SSE, donated seed samples to improve Heritage Farm's collection, and helped with the selections for our seed catalogs.

Carolyn systematically sends seed for trial to seed companies, including Southern Exposure Seed Exchange, Johnny's Selected Seeds, Tomato Growers Supply, Pinetree Garden Seeds, and Shepherd's Garden Seeds, with the hope that wide dissemination will lead to more interest in heirlooms and increased membership for SSE. For four years Carolyn coedited and published *Off the Vine,* a newsletter devoted exclusively to all aspects of heirloom tomatoes: history, folklore, seed saving, favorites, isolation distances, and growers of note. She planned and personally developed an 1850s vegetable garden for the nearby Shaker Historical Society. And she has been the maven for the tomato folder of America Online for four years, and is still going strong.

During the last decade, Carolyn Male has grown and evaluated more than 1,000 varieties of heirloom tomatoes, and this extraordinary book describes 100 of her favorites. Gardeners everywhere are blessed that Carolyn is sharing her vast knowledge of heirloom tomatoes as freely as she has always shared her seeds.

— KENT WHEALY
Executive Director
Seed Savers Exchange
January 1999

Cultivating an Heirloom Tomato Obsession

Tomatoes are the most widely grown fruit in the home gardens of America. The average grower usually buys whatever plants are available at the local nursery, or orders seeds of the newest hybrids, and the crop usually consists solely of red tomatoes. But a whole new world emerges—one with fruits in almost all colors of the rainbow, and tastes that range from transcendent to otherworldly—once the gardener discovers one of nature's sublime treasures: heirloom tomatoes.

The best of the heirlooms far exceed the hybrids when it comes to taste, and that's what tomatoes are all about—drippy, delicious, mouthwatering taste. Growing heirlooms can easily become an obsession, but a healthy one. It happened to me many years ago—don't be surprised if it happens to you.

The pool of heirloom tomato varieties gets bigger by the day; the Seed Savers Yearbook now lists several thousand. Over the past decade, I've grown more than 1,200 varieties of heirloom tomatoes, and it was not an easy task to select 100 of those for the Field Guide of this book. My criteria were based primarily, but not exclusively, on taste. Some varieties were chosen purely for their popularity; others, because they represent a certain class, fruit shape, or wild coloration. But all are distinctive, and worth trying in your garden.

As you delight in the harvest of your first heirloom tomatoes, keep in mind that taste is not only personal, but can vary for the same variety from garden to garden and year to year—soil type, weather, and climate can profoundly affect a tomato's flavor, and also its appearance. Marizol Gold, a gold-red bicolor, can have tangy sweet taste in my zone 5 garden one year, and be quite bland the next. Seed sources also have an impact on the characteristics of a given tomato. If your seeds are far removed from the source of origin (or if they were collected improperly), you may end up with a tomato that has developed subtle differences due to mutations that have altered it from the original strain.

My aim with this book is to not only convey everything I know about sowing, growing, and cultivating heirloom tomatoes, but also to offer a glimpse into the wonderful history and lore attached to so many varieties. Mortgage Lifter, for example, was so named because the sale of seedlings by its creator ended up paying off his mortgage.

As your knowledge grows, hopefully you'll want to share your experiences (and seeds) with others. You may even find that spreading the word about heirloom tomatoes is as satisfying as watching them grow in your garden. Spreading the word certainly has been my mission—and passion—ever since I became obsessed with heirloom tomatoes those many years ago.

—CAROLYN J. MALE
January 1999

ORIGINS
of the TOMATO

There are nine species of tomato in the genus *Lycopersicon,* and all but two are inedible, small, hard green fruits. The well-known garden tomato, *Lycopersicon esculentum,* is more correctly classified *L. lycopersicon,* but both names are found in tomato literature. The other edible species, *L. pimpinellifolium,* is known as the "currant tomato" because of its small size. Not only are the other seven species inedible, but the seeds of at least one of them has to go through the digestive tract of a turtle before they can germinate. All nine tomato species originated in the high coastal mountain regions of Chile and Peru. The Spanish conquistadores were the first to write about the tomatoes they saw being cultivated for food in Mexico during the sixteenth century.

The Spanish were responsible for disseminating the seeds to the Philippines (where they spread to all of Southeast Asia), the Caribbean, Italy and Spain, and from there, to the rest of continental Europe. The first tomatoes described were yellow —red tomatoes and the brilliantly colored hues that many people now associate with heirloom varieties (oranges, bicolors, pinks, greens, ivories, black-reds, black-pinks, and whites) appeared later in tomato history.

Tomatoes in the continental United States were first written about by a visiting Englishman, William Salmon, who saw them growing in "Carolina" in the late 1680s. It isn't clear whether these tomatoes came from the Caribbean or spread from Mexico at an earlier

Cherry tomatoes, like those edging this border, are a staple in any serious heirloom tomato grower's garden.

date. Seeds for tomatoes were imported from France by Thomas Jefferson in the early 1780s, and were also being sold in Philadelphia by 1800, Baltimore by 1810, and Boston by 1827. In a few short years, tomato seeds were available virtually everywhere. In the 1830s, currant tomatoes *(L. pimpinellifolium)* were seen growing wild in southern regions of the United States.

By the mid 1800s, cherry-, pear-, plum-, and egg-shaped tomatoes were described. Also available were larger fruits, but they tended to be lumpy, bumpy affairs instead of the smooth-skinned varieties we crave today. Different colored tomatoes were also described during this time. Early farmers and gardeners improved the varieties available to them by natural selection; that is, when they saw an improvement in a particular variety, they saved the seeds, planted them, and thus obtained new varieties. In this simple way, there was continuous improvement in available tomato varieties.

Wherever tomatoes had been introduced by the Spanish, new

strains and varieties arose by mutation of the various genes (or by natural cross-pollination and subsequent dehybridization to an open-pollinated form, which means that a tomato's seed grows "true to type"). The changes occurred in shape, size, coloration, foliage, plant habit, and taste. Farmers and gardeners took advantage of these mutations, developing their own tomato varieties in the U.S., Europe, and elsewhere. Starting in the late 1800s, many seed companies started selling seeds to the public. The origin of those seeds is not always stated, but Alexander Livingston, an early tomato proponent, wrote a wonderful book that described the origin and development of the varieties released by the Livingston Seed Company before 1890.

The heirloom varieties that we recognize and grow today wouldn't have been possible without the selection techniques used by early farmers and gardeners to improve upon the fruit and foliage characteristics found in the earliest tomatoes. Many of these varieties have been passed down within families through the generations, while others were introduced by commercial seed companies. And new varieties are being created all the time from natural cross-pollination, deliberate pollination (by humans), and spontaneous mutation.

WHAT IS AN HEIRLOOM TOMATO VARIETY?

Some people say that heirloom tomatoes are treasured varieties, and have personal appeal regardless

TOMATO FOREFATHERS

Alexander Livingston, who owned a seed company in Ohio, was responsible for introducing many excellent varieties such as Paragon, Golden Queen, Acme, and Perfection. Many of those varieties are still with us, and you'll find Golden Queen listed in the Field Guide of this book.

Two varieties that most resembled our well-known round red tomatoes were Paragon, introduced by Livingston, and Trophy, developed by Dr. T. J. Hand by crossing a small cherry tomato with a larger, lumpy one. Seeds of Trophy were promoted by Colonel George Waring, and sold for 25 cents each in the 1860s.

of their place of origin or the first report of their existence. Others maintain that heirloom tomatoes must have been cultivated prior to 1940 because by the mid 1930s, many seed companies were starting to create hybrids by crossing two varieties, and so the introduction of hybrid seed to the public occurred soon thereafter. Still others argue that an heirloom tomato isn't a true heirloom unless it has been passed down from generation to generation within the same family or extended family. My sympathies lie with this camp.

The problem with "commercial" heirlooms is that one never knows the true origin of the variety. Was it selected for and propagated by the seed company? Or did they find it elsewhere, possibly improve upon it by selection, and then introduce it? Alexander Livingston, for example, states that he found the tomato he called Golden Queen at a farmer's fair and that it was probably once a family heirloom. But Livingston also states that he "improved" it before calling it Golden Queen and releasing it through his seed company.

Several seed companies bought up the rights to certain family heirlooms in the late 1930s and 1940s. One parent of the hybrid Big Boy is a case in point; it is a pink heirloom beefsteak from the Midwest. To me, the category that contains created tomato heirlooms lacks the lore and tradition I associate with family heirlooms. Often the parentage of these created heirlooms is not made public. In some cases we know that both parents were family heirlooms, but other possibilities have also been mentioned, including a hybrid. Lastly, some of these created heirlooms are now being created as hybrids, adding yet another dimension to the problem of defining an heirloom.

From a reproductive standpoint, all heirloom varieties are open-pollinated, which means that saved seed sown the next year will give you the same variety unless natural cross-pollination or spontaneous mutation occurs. Seed saved from hybrid tomatoes does *not* give rise to identical plants in the next generation.

CLASSIFICATION OF HEIRLOOM TOMATOES

Craig LeHoullier was the first to suggest that heirlooms could be classified into three groups: commercial heirlooms, family heirlooms, and deliberately created heirlooms. I've named a fourth group the "mystery group" because certain tomatoes don't fit into any of the aforementioned categories.

COMMERCIAL HEIRLOOMS. These varieties were introduced to the public by seed companies before 1940. Many of our current hybrids are derived from some of these wonderful old commercial varieties. Craig and I have spent a great deal of time searching out these varieties from the USDA tomato seed collection. Many were already available but we were able

T*his "heirloom" farmhouse serves as the backdrop for a colorful selection of freshly picked heirloom tomatoes.*

to identify several important new rescued ones such as Paragon (1870), Trophy (1870), Favorite (1883), Beauty (1885), Optimus (1885), Magnus (1900), and Alpha Pink (1915). (The dates in parentheses are the dates of commercial introduction.) We listed these in the Seed Savers Exchange (SSE) Yearbook in the early 1990s so that they would be available to gardeners interested in historic varieties, especially those associated with the creation and supervision of historic vegetable gardens. Of course, some other commercial pre-1940 varieties are available through the Seed Savers Exchange and certain specialty seed companies (see Appendix).

Other historic varieties we obtained from the USDA, which were listed infrequently in the SSE Yearbook and were generally unavailable to the public, included Green Gage (pre-1800), King Humbert (pre-1800), Early Large Red (probably pre-1800), Acme (1875), Triumph (1879), Alpha (1882), Early Ruby (1891), and Dwarf Stone (1902).

Not all of the heirloom tomato varieties have made it through the years with their genes intact—seeds of several varieties I received from the USDA were crossed. Matchless, a determinate variety (short and bushy, with tomatoes that ripen in a limited time period, typical of today's hybrids), had gorgeous rugose (puckered) foliage with the expected red oblate (flattened) fruit, but the tomatoes were mealy and the taste undistinguished. Another strain of Matchless I received several years ago from Dave Austin, however, had much better taste.

*A*ngora-type foliage, characterized by a grayish green color and a fuzzy surface, sparkles in the sun.

Redfield Beauty has been outstanding. Paragon and Optimus are also personal favorites, but Acme came through the years with a few genes altered—the strain I grew was mushy and tasteless. Released by the Livingston Seed Company in 1875, Acme was said to be the first truly smooth pink tomato. On the bizarre side, Livingston released a variety called Honor Bright in 1897. The foliage on this plant is mostly yellow, the blossom petals ivory white, and the small fruits change in color from light green to white to yellow to orange to red as they mature. With such a wide range of colored fruit, the plant is truly spectacular, but the fruits don't taste very good at all. Craig LeHoullier was able to make the connection between Honor Bright and the variety currently known as Lutescent.

FAMILY HEIRLOOMS. These are

the heirlooms that most people want to grow. Family heirlooms were initially selected for and genetically stabilized to an open-pollinated form by astute farmers and home gardeners. (The seeds of open-pollinated tomatoes produce plants and fruits that look exactly like the ones from which they came.) Many of these varieties were brought to America by immigrants as treasured family heirlooms during the late 1800s and early 1900s. And these family heirlooms are still arriving today. Several years ago I obtained seeds from a family that had newly immigrated from Moldova. The variety was named Sandul Moldovan to honor their heritage. Sandul Moldovan has become one of my favorite heirloom tomatoes. Other examples are Eva Purple Ball from the Black Forest region of Germany, Soldacki from Poland, Cuostralée from France, Marizol Gold from Germany, and Myona from Italy.

Of course, family heirlooms have also been developed and maintained in this country. A listing of American heirlooms might include Aunt Ginny's Purple, Cherokee Purple, Red Brandywine, Mortgage Lifter, and Kellogg's Breakfast. We know nothing of the origins or past history of most of these family heirlooms, but we can trace the lineage of a few varieties. Marizol

SEED SAVERS EXCHANGE

Seed Savers Exchange (SSE) was formed in 1975 by Kent and Diane Whealy with the intent of preserving older, mostly heirloom varieties of vegetables, fruits, berries, and grains. Diane had received seeds from her grandfather for an heirloom morning glory called Grandpa Ott's (brought from Bavaria in 1824), a pink heirloom tomato, and a bean variety. Kent and Diane realized that the older generation who saved seeds of heirloom varieties was passing on, and that younger generations were not interested in keeping those varieties alive by saving seed. Many varieties were being lost forever because no one was preserving them.

Starting with a membership of eight in 1975, the SSE grew quickly as people interested in preserving rare heirloom varieties joined the organization. Many members contributed their own heirloom seeds to be offered to others for preservation. The organization maintains seeds of heirloom varieties in Decorah, Iowa, where they are based. As of 1998, there were about 9,000 nonlisted members and about 1,000 listed members. The listed members offer their varieties in the annual Seed Savers Yearbook, and seeds can be requested from listed members by other members for a small fee. A coding system identifies some as varieties unavailable to nonlisted members. Membership costs $30 per year, and for that you receive the Seed Savers Yearbook, plus summer and harvesttime publications filled with informative articles. A separate seed catalog that also offers seed-related items such as books, postcards, and calendars is available to the general public.

T*he small yellow variety called Galina's looks robust on the vine and contrasts beautifully with its deep green potato-leaf foliage.*

Gold, a gold-red bicolor tomato, was brought from the Black Forest area of Germany to the U.S. in the late 1800s by the Bratka family. If you look at a current map of the Black Forest, there's a town called Maria's Zell, and it's possible that the name Marizol derives from there. (Marizol Gold also happens to be one of my favorite bicolor tomatoes.)

Thousands of family heirlooms are listed in the Seed Savers Yearbook and seeds for some of them are also available commercially. SSE has been a major force in encouraging people to locate these family heirloom varieties and to make them available to others.

But we must not assume that each variety is unique, because names do get changed and genes "wander." For example, I can plant out twenty large pink beefsteak tomatoes with potato-leaf foliage

(having no indentations on the leaf margin) and challenge anyone to identify them by variety name; they'd be unable to do so— although there may be subtle differences in color, taste, and growth habit.

CREATED HEIRLOOMS. The third group of "heirlooms" comprises varieties deliberately created by crossing either two known heirlooms or an heirloom and a hybrid. The initial hybrid seed has to be grown out for several generations to dehybridize it to an open-pollinated form. The number of generations necessary to dehybridize any variety is a function of the desired traits being sought, and ranges from three to ten years. Examples include Green Grape, Green Zebra, and Banana Legs, all bred and selected for by Tom Wagner of California, and introduced to the public through his now-defunct seed firm called Tater Mater Seed Company. Tad Smith of Pennsylvania has also created some nice varieties, such as Pale Perfect Purple and Snowstorm.

Many people maintain that if an heirloom is "created" by deliberate cross-pollination, it isn't a true heirloom.

MYSTERY GROUP. These are tomatoes that arise after a natural, not deliberate, cross-pollination between two varieties. Almost all heirlooms arose in this manner —in addition to spontaneous mutation—but the important distinction is that these are varieties selected for in modern times. These tomatoes are not true family heirlooms, although their parents were, and they aren't deliberately created heirloom tomatoes.

Several years ago, Craig LeHoullier sent out seed of Yellow Brandywine to an SSE member who had requested them. That fall he got back a picture showing large red beefsteak tomatoes with an orange undertone at the shoulders. Seed was also sent back with the picture. Clearly, the seed Craig sent out was crossed because Yellow Brandywine is a large yellow beefsteak with potato-leaf foliage. Since red is dominant over yellow genetically, we know the other parent must have been a red variety. Because I have unlimited growing space, I volunteered to

try to dehybridize the seed and obtain that red tomato in an open-pollinated form.

The seed Craig initially sent out was the hybrid seed (known as F1 seed) that resulted from an accidental crossing between Yellow Brandywine and an unknown red parent. The seed returned to him was F2 seed saved from the red beefsteak. Upon planting the F2 seed, I got yellow beefsteaks with regular foliage, pink beefsteaks with either regular foliage or potato-leaf foliage, and the red beefsteak with potato-leaf foliage. What a magnificent tomato that red beefsteak turned out to be. It took me five years to purify it, each year selecting for the red beefsteak and growing out the seed until all seed sown gave rise to identical red-fruited beefsteaks with potato-leaf foliage. We named this variety OTV Brandywine. The OTV stands for *Off the Vine,* the newsletter about heirloom tomatoes that Craig and I published for four years in the mid 1990s. The Brandywine part of the name came from the female parent, which was Yellow Brandywine. This variety is now available to the public.

There are many heirloom tomato aficionados who now are growing out seed from naturally crossed varieties—it's great fun and there are always surprises. How do you know when you have naturally crossed seed? When you plant seed for a specific variety and not all the plants grow true to form.

Selecting Heirloom Tomato Varieties

Nowadays, the novice heirloom gardener often ends up confused by the many choices of heirloom tomato varieties that have become available. Luckily, selection is often simplified by knowing what color or shape of tomato you wish to grow, the purpose for which the tomatoes are being grown, and where (in a geographical sense) the tomatoes are being grown. Some home gardeners want to grow only varieties for eating fresh (German Red Strawberry, Earl of Edgecombe, and Druzba are superb); others plan to make lots of sauce (Opalka and Heidi are two great-tasting paste types); still others grow for market sales (I highly recommend Box Car Willie and Eva Purple Ball); and some folks just want to grow the biggest tomatoes possible (blockbusters like Zogola, Cuostralée, and Omar's Lebanese).

About Zones

Regardless of your growing zone, you need to sow your seed indoors about six to eight weeks before the last frost date. (Gardeners in zones 9 and 10 should grow two crops each year to avoid the summer heat.) Specific directions on seed sowing are given in the next chapter.

Zone 3. Since there are as few as 60 to 70 frost-free days in some zone 3 areas, the varietal choices

*A*lthough not a true dry-fleshed paste tomato, the variety Amish Paste is a popular midseason heirloom.

for zone 3 growers are limited. They should be able to grow all the early varieties, and some of the mid-season varieties *if* they start seed indoors very early, set out larger-than-normal transplants, and protect them from frost.

ZONES 4, 5, AND 6.

Gardeners in these zones have the best selection of heirlooms that will grow well. Gardeners in zone 4 will have to start their plants earlier and protect them with Walls O' Water, wrap the cages, or provide frost protection as they normally do in the late spring. Zone 4 gardeners may also have trouble maturing some of the very long season varieties, such as most bicolors and the larger-fruited beefsteaks.

ZONES 7 AND 8.

Heirloom tomatoes in these growing zones can suffer from problems with blossom set and pollination because of the high, sustained summer heat. Fusarium wilt also becomes a problem here for many gardeners. Verticillium wilt and fusarium wilt are two common systemic fungal diseases (systemic diseases usually infect all plant parts). Although verticillium wilt is seen most often in northern zones, such as 4, 5, and 6, it's nowhere near as prevalent as fusarium wilt, which can be a major problem in zones 7 through 10. Variety selection will depend on what does well in your area because little recorded information exists on the tolerance of heirlooms to these wilt diseases.

Cherry tomatoes, however, almost always grow well in these zones. Overall, medium-size varieties tend to do better than large-fruit varieties because the latter have more problems setting fruit in areas with high temperatures and/or high humidity. The more unusual varieties, such as whites, greens, and blacks, also do well in these zones.

ZONES 9 AND 10.

Very high, sustained heat in these zones makes it necessary for tomato growers to sow two crops each year. This way, the summer heat that hinders good pollination can be avoided. The most heat-sensitive varieties should usually be transplanted to the garden in late January to early February, after the frosts of mid January have passed. The second crop should be transplanted to the garden in September. The most heat-sensitive varieties should be grown in the spring, but only experience will help you decide which ones to grow during which time periods.

MAKING CHOICES

When deciding which heirloom tomatoes to grow, keep a few generalizations in mind. Medium-size heirlooms are the most prolific, while heart-shaped varieties are the least prolific but yield some of the best-tasting fruits. Certain varieties have trouble setting fruit (Pink Brandywine is notorious in this regard because it has malformed blossoms that don't pollinate well, especially in high, sustained heat). The black-red and black-pink varieties like Cherokee Purple, Cherokee Chocolate, Noir de Crimée, and Black from Tula all color up and taste better when grown in the South. Cherry tomatoes, on the other hand, will grow and prosper almost anywhere. Red-gold bicolors are visually gorgeous but may suffer extensive concentric

THE ADAPTABLE TOMATO

The geographic origin of a tomato variety has no bearing on whether it will do well in a specific zone. Occasionally, a particular variety just doesn't perform up to expectations. If this happens, save the seed from the tomato fruits and plant them the next year. This technique is called "adaptation," and several explanations have been given for why it sometimes works. The most plausible is that mycorrhizae—mutually beneficial fungi that coexist with many crops—might have regional strains and thus require adaptation to the new area. Of the more than 1,200 varieties I've grown, adaptation was needed with only two.

There has been some discussion about adaptation of varieties in terms of disease tolerance, but this would require genetic mutation. Adaptation is usually considered to be a function of the environment. If a variety is grown the first year and is susceptible to disease, there is really no reason to expect it to perform differently in future years if the same pathogens are in the area, because disease tolerance can only be acquired by genetic mutation of the genes. And since many genes are involved in each systemic disease, this is unlikely to happen.

Tomatoes grown in wire cages made from concrete-reinforcing wire are mulched with red plastic and watered with drip irrigation.

cracking, and they are prone to soft flesh that rots easily. Also, certain bicolor varieties require a very long growing season and can only be grown reliably in the South. Three that perform well for me are Regina's Yellow, Marizol Gold, and Big Rainbow.

EARLY VARIETIES.

Friendly contests often occur among tomato growers to see who gets the first fruits of the season. Competition aside, the taste of most early varieties—whether they are hybrids or heirlooms—just isn't very good compared to the later-maturing varieties.

In most areas, early varieties should mature within 55 to 65 days. "Days to maturity" refers to the approximate time between transplanting to the garden and the appearance of ripe fruit. The exact time of maturity is completely dependent on the gardener's cultural practices and the weather. Occasionally, some of my mid-season varieties mature before the early varieties, but it's rare. Early-maturing variety suggestions might include Sophie's Choice, Azoychka, Matina, Anna Russian, Stupice, Jaune Negib, and Jaune Flammée. The latter two, although quite tasty, tend to be particularly susceptible to early blight, which is one of the most common fungal foliage pathogens. All early varieties are more susceptible to early blight than are later varieties.

PASTE TOMATOES.

There is absolutely no reason why gardeners should grow only standard pear and plum tomato types for paste. They are very susceptible to blossom end rot, and this is true for both hybrids and heirlooms. Blossom end rot is a condition that causes the bottom of the fruit to develop a dark black leathery area. Most paste tomatoes don't have great taste, so I suggest that any other good-flavored, solid-fleshed tomatoes be used. Actually, any variety can be used for paste if you just cook the tomatoes down a bit more to get rid of the excess juice. For the traditionalists, suggestions include Opalka (really outstanding), Martino's Roma, Tadesse, Wuhib, Amish Paste (large), and Heidi. Large solid-fleshed tomatoes include Andrew Rahart's Jumbo Red, Russian #117, and Aker's West Virginia.

VARIETIES FOR NOVICES.

The varieties listed below have shown great adaptability and performance in a range of geographical areas, as well as good foliage- and systemic-disease tolerance (see page 23). Of course, tolerance to disease depends greatly on where you live, the local prevalence of pathogens, and how you space and grow your plants. Varieties for novices include Eva Purple Ball, Druzba, Red Brandywine, Cherokee Purple, Aunt Ruby's German Green, Box Car Willie, German Head, and the potato-leaf varieties OTV Brandywine, Yellow Brandywine, Lillian's Yellow Heirloom, and Aunt Ginny's Purple. Very large-fruited varieties include Omar's Lebanese, Cuostralée, and Zogola. All cherry tomatoes also perform well, making them excellent for beginners.

FOR MARKET GARDENERS.

Market gardeners should be familiar enough with their heirlooms to educate the customer. Perhaps the biggest mistake I see is folks expecting to harvest and sell heirloom tomatoes the first year. It's wise to trial-grow many different varieties and see what works best in your climate and with your growing conditions before attempting to sell in a market situation. The following varieties are reliable with regard to yield and disease tolerance, depending on where you live. Good varieties to try first include Druzba, Box Car Willie, Eva Purple Ball, Mule Team, Lida Ukrainian, Red Brandywine, Break O' Day, and Redfield Beauty. These reach the 8-ounce to 1-pound range when grown well. The most reliable heart-shaped varieties include German Red Strawberry, Orange Strawberry,

Reif Red Heart, and Nicky Crain. Good orange varieties are Kellogg's Breakfast and Earl of Edgecombe, while good yellow to gold varieties are Dixie Golden Giant and Golden Queen.

VARIETIES FOR SELLING TO CHEFS.

It seems that more than anything else, chefs love a rainbow of heirloom cherry tomatoes. Recommended varieties include Mirabell, Red Pear and Yellow Pear, Dr. Carolyn, Amish Salad, Pink Ice, Green Grape, Riesentraube, Mini Orange, and Pink Ping Pong.

When selling to chefs, bring a sampling of colors and shapes and allow them to taste and work with the different varieties. Some chefs love the heart-shaped heirlooms, like Orange Strawberry, German Red Strawberry, and Nicky Crain, while others are drawn to the more exotic colors of White Queen, Noir de Crimée, Aunt Ruby's German

*Y*ellow Pear plants bear adorable tiny fruits in abundance. They are perfect served whole in a salad.

A *1929 Ford pickup truck is loaded with antique flats and a basket filled with heirloom tomatoes ready for delivery.*

Green, and Green Zebra. Reliable red-gold bicolors are Regina's Yellow and Marizol Gold. Interesting shapes such as Plum Lemon, Opalka, and Amish Paste might also be offered. Some chefs want just paste tomatoes, while others simply want the best-tasting heirlooms regardless of color or shape. But the cherry tomatoes remain the high-priced favorites.

FOR ORGANIC GARDENERS.

Organic growers have one major problem: foliage diseases (see page 26). It doesn't matter if you're an organic or non-organic gardener if your plants become infected with systemic diseases such as fusarium wilt, verticillum wilt, or root knot nematode—because there are no preventive sprays or cures available. If your plants do become infected with one or more of the many foliage diseases, copper-based sprays, which are not very effective, are all you have to combat them with. Proper spacing of plants in the garden helps fight this problem by increasing air circulation around the plants. Some tomatoes have shown good foliage-disease tolerance, especially the potato-leaf varieties. Suggested varieties include Druzba, Eva Purple Ball, Cherokee Purple, Red Brandywine, and Zogola. Potato-leaf varieties include Olena Ukrainian, Yellow Brandywine, OTV Brandywine, and Soldacki.

GROWING HEIRLOOM TOMATOES

T he culture of heirloom tomatoes is no different from the culture of hybrid tomatoes. In all respects—sowing, transplanting, and setting out—they're grown exactly alike. This fact, however, doesn't prevent a wide range of opinion about how to grow them. The real debate among tomato growers concerns practices such as pruning and fertilization, and whether to stake plants, cage them, or let them sprawl.

One common misconception about heirloom tomatoes is that they are more disease prone than hybrid varieties. From years of experience, I can tell you that this is simply not true. Heirloom tomatoes do suffer from some diseases, but no more than or different from those you will encounter with commercial hybrid varieties.

Tomato transplants set out in the garden while the weather is still unsettled don't do well, so it's very important to be sure that your average last-frost date has passed. I go two weeks beyond the date to ensure that my plants encounter favorable temperatures. (The average last-frost date in my zone 5 area is about May 15, and I don't set out plants until about June 1.) One year we had a killing frost on the Friday of Memorial Day weekend, and I almost lost all of my plants. Since that time, I have never rushed the season. But if you have just a few plants that you can protect from frost, you can take more chances than I can, because there is no way I can protect 500 to 600 plants in the field. Of course, there are those growers who want to transplant outside very early and use Walls O' Water or

E*merging seedlings unfurl their cotyledons. These will be followed by the first set of true leaves.*

other protection from frost in order to hurry along the first fruits. Although my experience is that the plants just don't do that well when planted out early, others have had good success—experimentation is the answer.

SEED SOWING

For most growers, seed should be sown indoors approximately six to eight weeks before the average last-frost date. If you don't know your last-frost date, call your local Cooperative Extension Service. Cherry tomatoes grow very fast and can be sown a week later than other varieties.

I prefer to sow seeds in seed pans, which hold ten to twenty different varieties. This way, they can be moved easily to control germination conditions rather than dealing with many individual small pots or cells. An 8-inch square Permanest pan with no drainage holes works best for me. The mix used for seed germination should *not* contain soil because soil con-

tains spores of fungi that can cause damping off, a disease that kills young plants just as they germinate. Jiffy Mix, Pro-Mix, and similar brands of soilless mix are excellent. Thoroughly moisten the soilless mix in a large container before packing it into the seed pan. Make shallow rows about ⅛ inch deep with a pencil, and sow seeds about ⅛ inch apart, then cover with mix. The rows should be spaced about 1 inch apart. In one 8-inch Permanest pan, I plant five rows with four varieties in each row. Three-inch plastic labels marked with a pencil identify each variety.

After sowing, take a small box and gently but firmly tamp down the mix so that it makes good contact with the seeds. The seed tray should then be slipped inside a plastic bag with one end propped open for good air circulation. Place the entire tray on top of a fluorescent light fixture (if you have a light set up), on top of a water heater or refrigerator, or any place where there will be heat to warm the bottom of the tray. Tomato seeds do not require as much bottom heat as peppers do, but they will germinate faster with it. You should not have to water until the plastic bag is removed because the plastic bag ensures retention of moisture. Germination will probably occur in three to seven days, but different heirloom varieties do have different germination times. Mirabell, for example, requires about two weeks to germinate.

At the first sign of germination, take off the plastic bag and put the pan under fluorescent lights, which should be positioned about 2 inches above the plants. Leave the lights on for sixteen hours a day and use one cool and one warm light tube. Once the plastic bag is off, water carefully but don't give the plants any fertilizer until two weeks after they have been transplanted from the seedling pan to cells. The first little "leaves" to emerge are not true leaves—they're technically known as the cotyledons. When the second set of leaves appears (these are true leaves, and plants will be about 2 inches high), it's time to transplant. Occasionally, you'll see a seed coat that has stuck to an emerging plant so the leaves can't unfurl. If this happens, moisten some cotton, hold it tightly to the seed coat, then gently try to remove the seed coat with tweezers.

Transplanting is important because it shocks the plant and forces it to develop roots. I transplant into plastic four-packs that have 2-inch cells. The transplants should be set deeply so just the leaves are above the level of the mix. Diluted liquid fertilizer can be used about two weeks after this initial transplanting. (It must be diluted or you risk burning the newly forming root system.) A few varieties will develop brown edges along the lower leaves at this stage, and the problem will spread from plant to plant. Most often this is seen with varieties that have wispy foliage. Simply pick off the diseased foliage. Once the plants are outside, they grow out of the problem.

When plants are about 9 to 12 inches high, they should be hardened off. This process slowly acclimates plants to sunlight, wind, and

GROWING IN NATURAL LIGHT

It's very hard to grow good, stocky tomato seedlings without artificial light, but many growers have no other options. Place newly transplanted seedlings in a south- to west-facing window to get the maximum light. If cold air comes in under the windowsill, block it off with some type of barrier. Cold air plus wet soil or foliage is a disaster in the making for fungal diseases. Since plants will bend toward the light (this is called phototropism), you need to turn the plants every day so that all sides of the plant receive equal exposure to the sun. Let the soil dry out a bit between waterings.

Despite your best efforts, seedlings will often become leggy and spindly. If this happens, they should be planted by the trench method (see page 21) after hardening off.

true outdoor conditions. Start by setting out transplants in a slightly shaded area, and then gradually moving them into the sun. It's best to stress the plants by not giving them too much water now (if they wilt, then water them); this is part of the hardening off process. Also during this time, be sure to remove any blossoms that might form— early plant growth in the garden should be directed toward root and foliage development, *not* reproductive development and the formation of fruit.

SITING THE GARDEN

Picking the right site for your heirloom tomato plants is crucial to their success. If you've grown tomatoes before, you probably have a good idea of where to put them. If you're new to tomato growing, select a site that has full sun, if possible. Tomatoes need a minimum of about six to eight hours of sunlight each day to grow well. It's also important that the plants be sited so that the early morning dew is burned off by the sun, which helps prevent foliage-disease development.

Tomatoes typically thrive in loam-type soils, but they can also be grown in sand- or clay-type soils. Soil preparation should start the preceding fall when the soil is rototilled or turned over by hand, especially if tomatoes or potatoes were grown at the site that summer. All plant debris should be removed, and the soil turned over as deeply as possible to help ensure that spores of pathogens are buried deeply so they don't cause disease the next year. Some growers plant

a cover crop of winter rye or clover as a nitrogen source if the garden area is large enough for this to be done easily. In spring, the soil can be worked when the frost is out of the ground and a handful of soil crumbles but does not form a ball. (Working soil that is too wet causes it to become compacted, which prevents oxygen, nutrients, and water from reaching plant roots.) Rototilling the soil again in the spring allows the soil to become fluffy and porous. If a cover crop has been grown, it's important to turn over that green material as soon as is possible to let it decompose before your final preparation of the garden.

SOIL AMENDMENTS

If you are preparing an area for the first time, it might be advisable to take a soil sample for analysis at your local Cooperative Extension Service. They will tell you if the pH is right (a pH value of 6 to 7 is fine), and whether or not you need to add something to raise or lower the pH. If you are low in any minerals, the report will also tell you what to add.

Organic gardeners usually add a few inches of compost in the spring, and work that thoroughly into the soil. Some growers prefer to spread an all-purpose fertilizer such as 5-10-10 (nitrogen/phosphorus/potassium) on the whole garden and work that into the soil. I prefer to fertilize the plants directly. It's a matter of observing how your plants grow, and adjusting your fertilizing techniques.

*P*lastic cells cut in half show the proper depth at which seedlings should be transplanted.

SPRAWLING, STAKING, CAGING, AND POT CULTURE

Regardless of how you grow tomatoes (staking, caging, and sprawling are the most common methods; some folks trellis their tomatoes or grow them in pots), you need to allow enough room between plants to ensure that there's no competition for water, oxygen, nutrients, and space for vine growth. Plants grown too close together will not thrive, and tangled vines make access to the plants and harvesting of the fruits very difficult. The method you use will usually depend on whether the tomato variety is determinate or indeterminate.

Determinate varieties (including most of the newer hybrids) are short and bushlike, have a shorter fruiting period as compared to indeterminate types, and do not need to be caged or staked. They are excellent grown in pots.

Indeterminate varieties are vining in nature, produce fruit until frost, and may be staked, caged, or allowed to sprawl. (Some people have grown them in *very* large pots.) Often the method used depends on the room available. Staking requires the least amount of space, followed by caging, then sprawling.

SPRAWLING. If you have unlimited growing space, there's nothing wrong with letting the plants sprawl—that's the way they grow naturally. Space them at least 3 feet apart in all directions. I grow my plants this way in 200-foot-long rows, with plants spaced 3 feet apart within the row, and leaving 5 feet between the rows to allow for mechanical cultivating and fertilizing.

Sprawling requires the least amount of labor because there are no cages or stakes to construct and erect, and no need to continually

G*rowing tomatoes using a trellis system usually requires more permanent structures than those used for staking or caging.*

tie up vines or push foliage back into the cages. You may lose the fruit that makes contact with the ground from rotting, but mulching can cut down on that loss.

STAKING. If your space is very limited, then staking might be appropriate. Staked tomatoes should be planted at least 2 to 3 feet apart. As the vines grow, you need to continually tie them to the stake. Be sure to drive stakes at least 1 foot deep into the ground to prevent them from toppling over in bad weather, especially as the foliage becomes heavy.

CAGING. Most growers with limited space who don't have the room to allow their plants to sprawl, or those who want to ensure that the fruit don't make contact with the ground, elect to cage their plants.

Cages should not be the conical metal varieties available at most hardware stores because they are too flimsy and will topple over with heavy plant growth, high winds, and rain. The best cages are homemade from concrete-reinforcing wire, and have a diameter of about 22 to 24 inches. Bamboo poles woven between the metal squares will securely anchor the cages to the ground. As with staked tomatoes, cages should be spaced about 2 to 3 feet apart.

POT CULTURE. Many growers have successfully grown heirloom varieties in pots. The short, bushy, determinate-type varieties are probably most appropriate, but there are only a few of these heirloom varieties and most of them are early maturing. Thus most pot-culture heirloom growers use larger pots to grow the indeterminate varieties, which make very large plants. The minimum container size should be 10 gallons, but 15 gallons is even better. Soil for the pots can be regular potting soil or soilless mix, which does dry out faster than regular potting soil.

Pot-grown plants require more water and more fertilizer than tomato plants grown other ways, so a moisture meter placed in the soil might be helpful. If the plants are in direct sun all day long, you'll probably need to water them twice a day, but be sure the soil has dried out between waterings. Since pot-grown plants will usually be indeterminate varieties (for the reason given above), some growers try to stick stakes into the pots and tie up the foliage as the vines grow. Others let the plants sprawl outward from the pot. Again, experimentation will allow you to determine what works best under your growing conditions.

TRANSPLANTING

Once the weather has calmed and the plants have been hardened off, it's time to transplant them. When you set the plants out, remember to set them very deeply, planting the stems right up to the new leaf growth. Remove any yellow leaves, and be sure to remove all blossoms. Remember, the first few weeks in the garden the plants should be forming good roots and foliage, and that energy would be diverted into early fruiting if you left the blossoms on.

If your plants are spindly or leggy instead of stocky and compact, and are unable to stand upright on their own when planted, then consider trenching them. Dig a shallow trench (about 4 to 6 inches deep) and lay the plants on their sides in the trench, being sure to leave the top of the plant above ground at one side of the hole (you may have to bend the top a bit, but it will grow upright in a few days). Tomatoes are somewhat unique in forming roots all along stems in contact with soil, so your plant will form a nice root system this way. Some growers prefer to trench

After hardening off and after its blossoms have been removed, this proper-sized plant of 9 to 12 inches is transplanted to the garden.

all their tomato plants, not just the spindly ones. I prefer to trench only the spindly plants because I prefer a deeper root development than is formed with trenching.

Some growers like to plant out very early and initially protect their seedlings with Walls O' Water; these use solar heat to warm tubes filled with water, thereby shielding the tender plants from low nighttime temperatures. Other growers wrap the cages with polyethylene to accomplish the same thing.

I gave up trying to force early growth many years ago because most early varieties—hybrids or heirlooms—just don't taste that good compared to those that mature just a few weeks later. Also, most early varieties are determinate and don't produce well over the long summer season. As I said before, I don't even plant out in my zone 5 growing area until two weeks past the average last-frost date. The cold nights, harsh winds, and rain early in the season don't allow for good plant growth, and in my experience little is gained by planting out early.

FERTILIZATION

One of the biggest mistakes tomato growers make is to overfertilize. An overdose of fertilizer will cause too rapid plant growth, which encourages disease, delays blossom formation and fruit set, and can damage new roots. A good granular fertilizer is one with NPK (nitrogen/phosphorus/potassium) values of 5-10-5 or 5-10-10. Similar liquid fertilizer concentrations can also be used. Strict organic growers must utilize what has already been worked into the soil.

The most successful fertilizing schedule for me involves two applications—that's all. I fertilize two weeks after the plants are set out in the garden and then again when the fruits are setting. If conditions are extremely wet, you *may* want a third application. This depends on whether or not excessive rains have diluted the initial applications, so your decision will be based on local conditions. A single dose of foliage fertilizer, such as seaweed or fish emulsion, is also a good idea (applied sometime before the second granular-fertilizer application) because some growers feel that it promotes a thicker leaf epidermis, which can help prevent foliage diseases.

Many growers are curious about the potential benefits of various soil additives, especially Epsom salts (magnesium sulfate). If your soil is deficient in magnesium, which is rarely the case, then use it. Others ask about dropping match heads into the planting hole, but the form of sulfur on match heads cannot be used by any plants. Various other additives have been mentioned from time to time, but there's really no need for them. I put nothing in the planting hole except the plant. Tomatoes are very forgiving in their growth, and do well under a wide variety of soil conditions.

PRUNING

Pruning a tomato plant involves removing "suckers," which are the new growths between the stems. They appear wherever two stems come together to form a V-shape. Normally sane tomato growers

B *lossom end rot (BER), characterized by the distinctive black leathery area, rears its ugly head on this tomato.*

often come close to blows when debating the merits of pruning. Pruned plants have much less foliage than unpruned plants. Those who prune claim to reap larger fruit, but I have never experienced that. The way to get larger fruit is to take off almost all the small fruits and allow just one or two tomatoes per stem to develop. If space were very limited I could understand pruning staked tomatoes, but as a rule, I'm firmly against pruning. Plants need to photosynthesize to produce energy for root, leaf, and fruit growth. Therefore, by allowing all of the plant's foliage to thrive, the plant is better able to photosynthesize.

Since most growers also experience leaf loss from foliage diseases, I believe it's wise to have the maximum foliage possible. Additionally, sparse foliage cover can lead to sunscald (see page 28).

If one does choose to prune, a good use for suckers is to start new plants in those areas where fall-grown tomatoes are possible. Since this kind of reproduction is vegetative rather than sexual, you'll get an identical plant.

BIOTIC DISEASES

Every grower of heirloom or hybrid tomatoes has problems with diseases, depending on where plants are grown. Diseases that result from bacterial, viral, fungal, and nematode agents are called biotic diseases because a specific agent causes the damage. There are two types of biotic diseases: systemic and foliage.

I have not listed the Latin names for the biotic pathogens, nor have I described the specific leaf lesions or specific wilting patterns, since it is often very difficult for the home grower to make an accurate diagnosis, even after consulting a Web site or tomato-disease book. Diagnosis is best done by professionals.

SYSTEMIC DISEASES. Systemic diseases infect the entire plant and are usually more serious than foliage diseases, which primarily result from infection of the leaves and occasionally the stems. You can't prevent systemic diseases if the agents for those diseases are found in your area, and the varieties you've planted are susceptible. Some heirloom varieties are quite tolerant of some systemic diseases, but there is no definitive list of those varieties at this time.

When you look at the listings for tomatoes in a catalog, you'll often see an alphabetic designation, such as VFNT, after the name of a hybrid tomato and occasionally after the name of an open-pollinated (OP) tomato. These designations indicate that the variety has exhibited some degree of tolerance to a specific disease.

"V" stands for verticillium wilt, which is found primarily in zones 4 to 6. "F" stands for fusarium wilt, which is found primarily in zones 7 to 10. There are several different strains of the fusarium wilt, called f1, f2, and f3. Tolerance to the disease can involve any or all of those strains—that is, a variety of tomato tolerant to f1 and f2 could still be susceptible to f3. The strains f1 and f2 are found

S *plitting of fruits from excess moisture isn't limited to longitudinal and stem end cracking. The split in the tomato above is way below the stem end site for cracking.*

throughout the South, but f3 is mainly a problem in California and Florida as well as North Carolina and surrounding areas.

"N" stands for root knot nematode disease, which is a problem mainly in sandy soils in California, Florida, and other Gulf Coast states. "T" denotes tobacco mosaic virus, which is not a major problem for the home gardener, occurring mostly in commercial greenhouse growing. Verticillium wilt, fusarium wilt, root knot nematode disease, and tobacco mosaic virus are all systemic diseases.

Varieties of tomatoes with alphabetical designations have demonstrated some degree of disease tolerance in challenge tests conducted in a laboratory or field setting. To "challenge" a tomato variety means to deliberately expose it to a specific pathogen. Such tests cost about $200 per pathogen and are usually done for commercially hybridized varieties either in university or private laboratories. Varieties cannot be advertised as having specific tolerances without such challenge tests because of legal liability. In the experience of most home growers, the advantage of growing such tolerant varieties usually means a few weeks of growth gained over varieties without those designations.

Heirloom tomatoes also have a range of tolerance to these same systemic diseases, but since heirlooms are truly orphans, there is no one to pay for challenge tests. Rarely, therefore, are tolerances noted beside heirloom names in catalogs. An exception is provided by Dr. Jeff McCormack, who lists

The development of diseased foliage can be lessened by the use of anti-fungal sprays.

tolerances for some varieties in his Southern Exposure Seed Exchange Catalog, based on his own personal observations.

If your plants suddenly wilt, they may have verticillium wilt, fusarium wilt, or root knot nematode disease, depending on where you live. Plants will wilt if they are dry, but watering or rain will restore them. Wilting accompanied by yellow leaves that shrivel to brown almost always indicates a systemic disease. If you need help in identifying a specific disease, it's best to call your local Cooperative Extension Service. Sprays cannot prevent or cure these disease— fungal spores of fusarium and verticillium can stay in the soil for up to three years, so conventional wisdom suggests rotating your tomato location every few years. There are several tomato-disease books and Web sites with pictures to help with identification, but the problem with such pictures is that they

A white blistery lesion called sunscald appears when foliage is sparse or rearranged in such a way that fruits are suddenly exposed to the sun.

don't show a progression of lesions due to a specific agent. Thus, a definitive diagnosis is difficult to make.

FOLIAGE DISEASES. Those who have grown hundreds of heirloom tomatoes over the years know that they are no more susceptible to foliage diseases than hybrids are. This is important because many uninformed garden writers claim that heirloom tomatoes are disease prone. In truth, it's more a matter of variety selection. Pik-Rite is a wonderful-tasting tomato hybrid variety that is very susceptible to early blight. Jaune Flammée and Jaune Negib are good-tasting early heirloom varieties that are also quite susceptible to this disease.

Early blight is the most common foliage disease nationwide. Septoria leaf spot, gray leaf spot, bacterial speck, and bacterial spot are also very common in many areas. All these diseases will defoliate the plant from the bottom up, but usually a harvest is obtained. (Plants suffering from systemic diseases, however, tend to die rather quickly.)

Disease prevention starts with adequate spacing between plants to allow for good air circulation, which inhibits germination of spores and bacterial growth when conditions are wet. Tomato pathogens thrive in wet conditions, so siting the garden where morning dews are burned off by the sun is very important, as is *not* watering at night unless you use drip irrigation. The point is to keep the foliage dry between waterings. The importance of using a light hand with fertilizer also cannot be overemphasized (see page 22).

Yellow leaves at the bottom of the plant early in the season are normal, but if those yellow leaves and the green leaves higher up on the plant show black or brown lesions or spots, you're dealing with a foliage disease. Foliage diseases are caused by either fungi or bacteria, and unfortunately there are no sprays available to the home gardener to fight bacterial foliage diseases. If foliage diseases appear, it's best to spray with a good antifungal such as Daconil or Bravo. Many growers don't even wait for symptoms to appear—they start a regular preventive program of spraying soon after the plants are transplanted. In general, the most common bacterial foliage diseases are less devastating than the fungal ones, and a harvest is usually possible.

Late blight is the only foliage disease that is deadly. The plant will be a mass of black, rotting foliage within one week of the onset of the disease, and no sprays will help at that point. Late blight is increasing in frequency across the country and is found along the eastern seaboard at higher inland elevations, in the Midwest and Pacific Northwest, and now in California. Very often the source is infected potato cull piles, but the spores can travel a great distance. Commercial farmers have access to some preventive sprays but the home gardener does not. Daconil or Bravo are the best preventives for late blight, but they are not as effective as they are against the other foliage diseases. It is important to realize that although early blight usually appears early in the season, it can appear at *any* time. The same is true for late blight.

Along with several other heirloom tomato growers, I've observed that potato-leaf and rugose-leaf (puckered-foliage) tomato varieties appear to withstand foliage diseases far better than most regular-leaf varieties. This may be because the leaf epidermis on these types is thicker and forms a stronger barrier to infection than that of regular-leaf varieties. One study done by Master Gardeners in Maryland compared regular-leaf hybrid varieties (with and without resistance to early blight) to Olena Ukrainian, an heirloom potato-leaf variety. Olena Ukrainian suffered the least amount of defoliation by far.

ABIOTIC DISEASES

Abiotic diseases are due to specific environmental or genetic conditions and are especially annoying. There's nothing worse than seeing black spots on the bottom of the fruit or cracks around the stem when you've tenderly sown and raised your plants, fertilized them, and kept them watered. For some of these conditions, there are preventive measures you can take, but for most of them there are not.

BLOSSOM END ROT. The one condition that seems to bother home gardeners most is blossom end rot (BER). It's often seen on the first green fruits as they start to get larger, and on fruits that are in the process of turning color. BER accelerates ripening, so it isn't uncommon to reach for that first mature fruit and find a black bottom—the dark, leathery spot appears on the blossom end, not the stem end. Luckily, this is not an infectious disease, and can't spread to other plants.

Stresses early in the season promote the development of BER; these include too much fertilizer (causing too rapid plant growth), uneven delivery of moisture, and high winds (which cause drying). Any or all of these stresses cause calcium to leave the fruit and go into the main part of the plant, and this lack of calcium in the fruit allows the black spot to develop.

In past years, it was thought that the addition of some form of calcium to the soil would prevent BER, but more recent research suggests that this is not true because the entire plant is not calcium deficient. Calcium sprays have been used on the fruit, but they don't work because calcium can't be absorbed through the skin of the tomato. If your soil is known to be calcium deficient, which is quite rare, you might want to add a small amount, but adding calcium does not prevent BER.

Thankfully, BER usually disappears as the season progresses, probably because larger plants can withstand the many stresses that induce BER. Not all varieties of tomatoes are equally susceptible —paste tomatoes are the most vulnerable. Because growing conditions influence the development of BER, it's best to try different varieties. The two most important things you can do to prevent this disease are to ensure even delivery of moisture by mulching, and to avoid overfertilizing.

SUNSCALD. When foliage cover is inadequate, tomatoes exposed to the sun will often develop sunscald, a large white, shiny, blistery area on the portion exposed to the sun. This disease is even more likely to occur if tomatoes first develop with an adequate foliage cover and then the foliage is rearranged or pruned, exposing the fruits to direct sunshine.

Prevention rests with selecting varieties that maintain a good foliage cover and by not rearranging or pruning the vines heavily as the fruits near maturation. Both immature and mature fruits can suffer from sunscald. In my opinion, tomatoes with sunscald are not edible.

CATFACING. Catfaced tomatoes have abnormal shapes, and often show clefts and scars. Catfacing is more prevalent when pollination occurs during cool weather, and subsequent fruits develop abnormally. It cannot be prevented. Again, some varieties are more prone to catfacing than others, and this is best determined by trial and error under your growing conditions. Despite their unusual shape, catfaced fruits taste just fine.

CURLING LEAVES. The most common reason for curling leaves is that the tomato variety carries what is called the "wilty gene." This is perfectly normal—most modern hybrids have this gene. Other reasons why leaves curl include a heavy fruit burden, and too cool, too hot, too wet, or too dry growing conditions.

If the leaves aren't just slightly curled, but instead are curled all the way over to form a tube, check for aphids. Aphids feed on the plant's juices and will weaken it, so they need to be treated. Curled leaves alone have no effect on either plant growth or fruit development.

GREEN SHOULDERS. Many older tomato varieties, both heirloom and hybrid, have green "shoulders" when the rest of the fruit is ripe. A gene called the "uniform ripening gene" usually prevents this from happening.

Green-shouldered tomatoes may not be as beautiful as tomatoes that ripen right up to the stem, but they taste just fine. Since this is a trait that is genetically controlled, the condition is considered normal and neither plant growth nor fruit development is adversely affected

CONCENTRIC CRACKING. Many tomato varieties develop concentric rings of split tissue around the stem end. This is a genetic characteristic and can't be prevented (other than to select varieties that don't have the genetic trait).

The pattern of concentric cracking can be so unique that it can help identify an unknown variety. For that reason, and to show whether or not a variety exhibits concentric cracking, at least one tomato in most of the pictures in the Field Guide of this book shows the stem end. There is absolutely nothing wrong with the fruit, and the taste is fine. If you look very carefully, you'll see that scar tissue forms over the cracks. Only if there are heavy rains is there the possibility of the scar tissue opening up, allowing access to bacteria and fungi, which results in rotting.

LONGITUDINAL CRACKING. Any tomato variety, hybrid or heirloom, can develop fruits with longitudinal cracking, which means

*B*ulgarian #7 shows longitudinal cracking after heavy rains because the skin cannot expand to accommodate the increased water inside the fruit.

that the tomato splits from top to bottom. This occurs only on ripe fruits when there have been heavy rains or overwatering. The epidermis of the mature tomato can't expand anymore in response to the absorption of water, so the skin splits open. Tomatoes harvested before bacteria and fungi contaminate the split and initiate rotting are perfectly fine to eat or use in cooking.

SAVING SEED

Part of the fascination with family-type heirloom varieties is the way they've been perpetuated: saved seed cherished and grown by generation after generation. The technique of seed saving—like the varieties themselves—has been passed down over the years as the means to preserve treasured tomato varieties for future generations. In many ways, saving seed by fermentation is a rite of passage for heirloom tomato growers. Not until you've squished the fruits in your hands and grown accustomed to the particular smell involved with fermentation are you a true heirloom tomato aficionado.

Heirloom tomatoes are particularly appealing because, unlike with hybrid tomatoes, each seed produces a plant identical to the one from which it was harvested. Unless a spontaneous mutation has occurred, or there has been a cross-pollination, all open-pollinated varieties (when seed is saved properly) produce plants and fruits indistinguishable from the original variety. Spontaneous mutations (permanent changes in genes) do occur, but they rarely affect the flesh color of the fruits. The most common mutations affect leaves and skin color.

Cross-pollination, another method that fundamentally changes seeds, occurs when the pollen from one variety accidentally pollinates the blossom of another variety. Normally this doesn't happen because all tomatoes are self-pollinating and don't need help from insects for reproduction. When it does happen, the seed saved from fruit of cross-pollinated tomatoes will *not* give rise to the original plant.

POLLINATION

Tomato blossoms are called "perfect blossoms" because they contain

P*lastic cups contain the freshly squeezed contents of various-colored heirloom varieties being processed for fermentation.*

both male and female reproductive structures. The stigma is the female receptive organ. The pollen-bearing anthers normally reside above the stigma. As the blossom matures, the stigma grows upward and comes in contact with the pollen. The pollen grains land on the stigma and travel down through the style to the ovary, where each pollen grain fertilizes one egg, or female gamete. The ovary swells, grows, and becomes a new tomato filled with fertilized seeds.

The majority of tomatoes reproduce in this manner, but there are some exceptions. Some varieties have "exerted stigmas," which protrude beyond the anthers. They require insect pollination, and are easily cross-pollinated.

The rate of cross-pollination depends on the isolation distance of one variety from another, and on the frequency of insect pollinators. The most prolific pollinators are sweat bees, not bumble bees. Cross-pollination rates can range from zero to about 30 percent. You can expect a certain percentage of cross-pollination if you grow a number of varieties—5 percent is considered very good. This means that for every hundred varieties, about five will be crossed, and not always give rise to the original plant. If you replant saved seed and the resulting plants or fruits are not identical to the original variety, then you've got crossed seed.

ISOLATION DISTANCES

If you plan to save seed, you will need to separate tomato varieties. Different distances are recommended, depending on whom you consult. Commercial growers of heirloom seed need to obey the greatest isolation distances. For home use—when seeds will not be shared with others—a distance of 3 to 4 feet within a row, and 5 feet between rows, is usually adequate. Those distances work very well for me; my cross-pollination rate is about 5 percent, which is quite good.

An exception to this spacing

rule involves currant tomatoes (*L. pimpinellifolium*), which have exerted stigmas and will cross with all other varieties of the normal garden tomato (*L. esculentum*). Currant tomatoes must be grown *at least* ¼ mile away from other varieties.

FERMENTING TOMATO SEED

Seed is isolated from tomatoes by the process of fermentation. A number of ripe, disease-free tomatoes of the same variety should be selected for this process. Several tomatoes of the same variety are crucial in case a mutation or cross-pollination has occurred in one of the tomatoes; this precaution will ensure that you'll get at least some of the seeds you want.

Ideally, six to eight plants of each variety should be planted, and fruits for fermentation should be selected from the inside three or four plants to avoid cross-pollinated plants. Also, there are minute but real differences between the foliage and fruits of the plants of one variety, and selecting fruits from several plants keeps this genetic variability, which is desirable.

HOW TO FERMENT SEEDS

Fermentation is not absolutely necessary to get viable seeds to sow the next year, but it does lower the number of tomato pathogens associated with the seeds, remove the gel capsules, and eliminate a germination inhibitor found within the capsules. Many commercial seed companies ferment their seeds, and it's easy to do at home.

Fermentation of seeds is prac-ticed for almost all vegetables that have fleshy parts around the seeds. The seeds of vegetable varieties with "naked" seeds, such as peppers, squash, or beans, do not need to be fermented, although they may have to be treated in other ways. While fermentation of tomato seeds is messy and fruit flies abound—as do unique odors—it is a rite of passage for all tomato aficionados, especially if seeds are going to be shared with others (you certainly wouldn't want to pass along pathogen-contaminated seeds).

There are several variations on the basic fermentation method, and my method is one that works for me and many others.

I use clear, 1-pint deli containers for fermentation. You can scale down the process by using small clear-plastic cups. Label each container with the variety name on tape. Squeeze the inner contents of enough fruit of one variety into the deli container until it's about half full. Before proceeding to the next variety, be sure to rinse your hands and check under your fingernails for stray seeds.

Place the deli containers in a seedling tray about 22 × 11 inches, and set it out of the sun in a place where the ensuing ripe odor and accumulating fruit flies won't bother anyone, and where it won't be tipped over by critters like raccoons and skunks. After three to five days—depending on the temperature and the variety—you'll see a white fungal layer develop on the top of the tomato juice and seeds. Do not stir the mixture. Some sources do recommend stirring, but fermentation is an

PROCESSING SEED

Fermentation is an anerobic process that allows sugars to metabolize to acids. There are numerous advantages to fermenting heirloom tomato seeds: it decreases the number of possible seed-borne pathogens, removes a germination inhibitor present in the gel capsules, and produces squeaky-clean seeds. While the associated odors and fruit flies are not pleasant, fermenting seeds is a rite of passage for every tomato aficionado.

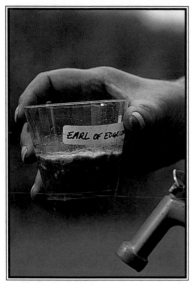

1 *Skim off the layer of white fungus, being careful not to remove any seeds in the process.*

2 *Slowly add water, allowing the seeds to settle. The good seeds will fall to the bottom.*

3 *Pour the colored liquid out, leaving only the seeds at the bottom.*

4 *Continue to add water and swirl the seeds until the water is clear.*

anaerobic (occurring without oxygen) process, and stirring introduces oxygen. Along the sides of the containers you'll see the bubbles of gas developing from the fermentation process.

The seeds should ferment for at least five days, longer if the temperatures are below 80°F in the daytime. Once the seeds have fermented adequately, sit with a pail in front of you and a pistol-grip hose nozzle in your hand. Pour out the top layer of white fungus into the pail, spritz some water into the container, and swirl it. The bad seeds will float; the good seeds will sink to the bottom. Continue this spritzing process until the water is clear and you can see the seeds at the bottom. If the seeds still have gel capsules around them, the fermentation process is not complete. If the seeds are a dark brown to black color, the fermentation has gone on too long, but the seeds are still viable and will germinate

well. Other methods suggest straining the mixture to isolate the seeds, but I've never had good luck with that because the strainer always clogs up.

The next step involves labeling paper (never plastic) plates with the variety names. Paper plates absorb the water on the seeds; plastic plates do not. Drain the water from the container, knock the seeds out onto a paper plate, and spread them around to form a single layer. If left in a pile, the seeds may germinate. Place the plates indoors, out of the sun, so that the seeds dry thoroughly. Depending on humidity levels, this may take up to a week or more. Finally, place the seeds in labeled, airtight containers—old pill bottles or film canisters are good—and store them under cool, dry conditions. Plastic seed vials for seed storage can also be purchased.

The seed containers can also be stored in a refrigerator, which

*A*lthough photographed here in the sun, paper plates with newly fermented seeds should be placed out of the sun for proper drying.

prolongs their viability, but once they are removed from the refrigerator, be sure to wait until the condensation disappears before you open the containers or the added moisture will actually decrease seed viability.

Seeds processed in the way I've described will remain viable, with at least a 50 percent germination rate, for five to seven years. If you need to store seeds longer, silica gel can be used to lower the moisture content of the seeds, thereby extending their viability. Silica gel and moisture-proof plastic vials can be ordered from places like the Southern Exposure Seed Exchange (see Appendix).

Some commercial seed producers use chemical methods to lower the number of seed-borne pathogens, but these chemicals are not generally available and are quite harsh.

The seeds you've saved will grow true to type if there have been no spontaneous mutations or cross-pollinations—and you'll have the satisfaction of knowing that you've preserved these open-pollinated heirlooms by doing just what tomato growers have been doing for hundreds of years.

Creating Your Own Heirloom Tomatoes

I f you thumb through a catalog that offers a wide selection of open-pollinated (OP) tomato varieties, you'll notice that many of them are named after individual people. The listings probably include varieties like Dr. Wyche's Yellow, Dr. Neal, Aunt Ruby's German Green, Aunt Ginny's Purple, and Crnkovic Yugoslavian. All of these are considered family heirlooms, presumably named after the family member who championed them. The unusual names and the history they represent—whether that history is known or not—are part of the lure of heirloom tomatoes.

What makes these plants truly special is that you can create your very own heirloom varieties. If you have the time and space, breeding your own tomato variety—with the traits and tastes that appeal to you—can be quite easy and rewarding. Then you can name offspring after your Uncle Joe, Aunt Agnes, Baby Matilda, or even yourself. (Yes, there is a Dr. Carolyn heirloom, but I accepted the honor after it had been named for me by Steve Draper.)

There are three common ways to create your own heirloom variety, and each can be done by the home gardener. The first method involves crossing two heirloom varieties, then selecting and genetically purifying their offspring into an open-pollinated form. Second, you might be able to identify a plant in your garden that has already been crossed naturally, and then dehybridize it to an open-pollinated form. A third method is to dehybridize a commercial hybrid. While all of these methods start differently, the way to "purify" tomato varieties is the same for all of them.

DELIBERATE CROSS-POLLINATION

There are two basic ways to cross-pollinate tomato plants. The first method described is considered by many the "proper" way. The second approach is decidedly more casual and unpredictable, but also has its merits.

Select any two varieties as parents. Keep in mind that the more dissimilar the parents—in terms of fruit color, shape, and foliage—

the more interesting the offspring will be. Choose one parent to be the recipient (female) of the pollen from the other parent.

Early in the day, select a newly opened blossom of the female parent. Using tweezers, carefully remove the pollen-bearing anthers, which will prevent the plant from self-fertilizing. (This step is trickier than it sounds, and should be practiced on a test blossom before doing it on the parent plant.) Then transfer the pollen from the anthers of the male parent to the stigma of the female parent. Do this by taking some pollen-bearing

M*y grandfather's "heirloom" wheelbarrow, a treasured keepsake, is the focal point for this collection of heirloom tomatoes.*

anthers in your hand and rubbing them against the female stigma. Another way to accomplish this is by using a clean cotton swab to gather the pollen and deposit it on the stigma. (This method is considered "proper" because you actually prevent the blossom from self-pollinating by emasculation, or removal of the pollen-bearing anthers.)

Contrary to popular opinion, there's no need to put an isolation bag over the now-fertilized baby tomato to protect the stigma from unwanted insect pollinators. There are many more pollen grains than ovules to fertilize, so possible visits by insect pollinators will usually not be successful. Some people, however, still like to protect the pollinated stigma with a protective covering of Reemay or a similar porous but insect-proof fabric. Last, attach a tag to the stem of the fertilized blossom for easy identification.

A more casual approach to crossing involves *not* removing the anthers from the female parent plant. Transfer pollen from the male plant as described above, but allow the female parent to self-fertilize. If the anthers are not removed from the female parent, then pollen from two sources might be involved. This way, all of the F1 (first generation) plants grown out from this cross may not be identical, which would be the case if you remove the anthers from the recipient blossom. Since the idea is to create new and interesting varieties, this method may give you more variety—but less control.

SELECTING FOR A NEW VARIETY

Keep tabs on the fertilized blossom, and shortly you'll see the ovary swell with a baby tomato. When the tomato is ripe, process the seeds by fermentation (see page 33). Plant these F1 hybrid seeds the following growing season. All the plants and fruits that result should be identical—*if* only one kind of pollen did the fertilizing. If two types of pollen were involved, you'll usually see more than one kind of plant in this F1 generation. In this second season, you won't be selecting plants because they should be identical if one kind of pollen was used for crossing. The "casually" pollinated plant may give you F1 seeds that result in more than one plant or fruit type. If so, make your selection(s) at that point. This season, all you want to do is harvest ripe fruit and save the seed, now called F2 seed.

In your third year, plant out as many of the F2 seeds as possible because you will see a big cross-section of plants and fruits. A wide range of different plants should emerge from this crop because the genes from the parents are sorting themselves out. It is from this crop that you will be selecting the plants to purify genetically.

Select a plant with fruit, foliage, and taste that appeals to you and save only that seed (now considered F3 seed) for next year. Plant the seed again, saving only seed from the plants that match the previous generation. You'll notice that other strains or plant types continue to appear, but select only for the strain or plant type you chose last year. Repeat this process year after year, until the strain you've selected grows from every seed that you've planted. At this point, the strain is considered open-pollinated and qualifies as a new variety. The process may take three to ten years, depending on the particular genetic traits involved.

Once you've created the variety, it's yours to name, brag about, and share with others. You can grow this new variety every year from saved seed as long as a chance cross-pollination or spontaneous mutation doesn't occur.

DEHYBRIDIZING A NATURALLY CREATED HEIRLOOM HYBRID

When you plant saved seed from a specific variety, a completely unexpected variety will sometimes result. Instead of the expected potato-leaf foliage with huge pink fruits, for example, you get plants with red globe-shaped fruits and regular foliage. If this happens, you can usually conclude that the variety was cross-pollinated naturally by insect pollinators in the previous year. Instead of getting upset, seize this opportunity to create your own heirloom.

The seed saved from the previous year that gave rise to the cross-pollinated plants was the F1 hybrid seed. Seed from the cross-pollinated plants is F2 seed—the initial cross-pollination has already been done for you. Simply plant the F2 seed and select the plant you want to purify, and continue growing it out until it stabilizes, as described above.

DEHYBRIDIZING A KNOWN COMMERCIAL HYBRID

If you grow a hybrid tomato that you really like, you can dehybridize it and select for its offspring. The seeds you save from the hybrid tomato are the F2 seeds. When you plant them, you'll see a variety of plant and fruit types. Ultimately though, the choices for selection will depend on the parents used to make the original commercial hybrid seed. After planting the F2 seed, select the plants you want to dehybridize and follow the steps explained above until you have an OP form.

GENETIC TRAITS FOR SELECTION

In addition to selecting tomatoes grown from F2 seed in terms of taste, fruit color, shape, and foliage, there are other characteristics you may want to consider when choosing among tomato offspring. Some growers want only the

IS A COMMERCIAL HYBRID REALLY A HYBRID?

There have been reports of F2 seeds saved from hybrids giving rise to plants that are alike, which means that there was no gene sorting. One conclusion is that the seed being sold as hybrid was not hybrid at all, but open-pollinated. Another explanation for this occurrence has to do with the parents of the hybrid. If identical plants result from F2 seed saved from commercial hybrids, perhaps the parents of the hybrid were very similar.

In the "casual" method of pollination, pollen from the blossom on the left (the male parent) is placed on the stigma of the blossom on the right (the female parent).

biggest tomatoes, and will save seed only from the biggest fruits generation after generation. You may want an earlier fruiting form of a known variety. One friend crossed Pink Brandywine with a number of early OP varieties in an effort to get an early fruiting variety with the superior taste of Pink Brandywine. This is an admirable effort because most experienced tomato growers agree that the majority of early fruiting varieties are short on taste. The point is to use your imagination when deciding what characteristics to select for in your own crosses.

HOW MANY PLANTS DO I HAVE TO GROW OUT?

The whole business of cross-pollinating and dehybridizing tomatoes can get very complicated if you wish to be more scientific than I have been in this chapter. In the book *Breed Your Own Vegetable Varieties* by Carol Deppe, there is a chart that indicates how many

plants you should grow in order to see most of the possible genetic combinations of plants and fruits from your crosses. However, it can be just as rewarding—and a bit less rigorous—to grow out as many plants as your space allows, and follow the genetic traits that result. A little luck also helps. One amateur hybridizer sent me F2 seed to grow out. He knew what genes were involved, and had calculated that one of sixty-four plants would have the desired characteristics. I grew out only eight plants the first year and found the desired plant and fruit. Yes, I got lucky, but you might, too.

TOMATO TRAITS AND GENETICS

You might recall from high-school biology that certain genetic traits are referred to as being either dominant or recessive. The genes of heirloom tomatoes are no different in this regard. The most scientific-minded tomato hybridizers factor in the basic traits when crossing tomatoes. By doing the same thing, you can make more educated choices when selecting parents for new varieties.

Red pigment—the color that represents "tomato" for many— is dominant over yellow, for instance. If you cross yellow fruit and red fruit, the F1 generation will bear red fruit. You won't see various combinations until the F2 generation. Potato-leaf foliage is a recessive trait, but it's possible to cross two varieties with regular-leaf foliage and get an offspring with potato-leaf foliage. In this case, there would have to be recessive potato-leaf genes in both parents of the cross.

Spontaneous mutations occur all the time. One gene that frequently mutates is the one responsible for skin color. If the skin is yellow and the interior of the tomato is red, the tomato will appear red. If the skin color mutates to clear colored, then the tomato appears pink, but the interior is still red. In fact, there is no difference between pink and red tomatoes other than their skin color.

At the end of the day, you don't need to love genetics to enjoy creating your own heirloom tomatoes. It's great fun, and you may end up with a tomato you can call your own. If you get addicted to making crosses, however, the reference books listed in the Appendix are great resources.

A KEY *to the* FIELD GUIDE

Photographs of the tomatoes in the Field Guide were taken in the summer of 1998 between mid August and mid September. The tomatoes were grown in my zone 5 garden in Loudonville, New York, with the exception of Aunt Ruby's German Green, Jefferson Giant, and Tiffen Mennonite, which were grown by Wayne and Debra Freihofer in Loudonville, New York.

TYPE refers to the classification of heirlooms as family, commercial, created, or mystery (see page 4).

ORIGIN refers to the country in which the heirloom was first seen.

MATURITY refers to the approximate number of days from transplanting a young plant into the garden until the appearance of its first mature fruits. In my zone 5 garden, early-season maturity usually occurs in 55 to 65 days; midseason maturity occurs in 65 to 80 days; and late-season maturity occurs in more than 80 days.

COLOR/SHAPE: Both qualities can be influenced by environmental conditions. Globe or globular refers to round tomatoes; oblate refers to flattened-globe tomato shapes; and beefsteak refers to large, more irregular shapes.

SIZE/ARRANGEMENT: Sizes are given in approximate ounces and pounds. Arrangement refers to growth habit of the fruits, such as "in clusters."

YIELD is based on my personal experience and the growing conditions in my zone 5 garden.

PLANT/FOLIAGE: Indeterminate habit refers to vining plants; determinate plants are bushlike. Regular-leaf foliage has indentations on the leaf margins; rugose foliage has a puckered, quiltlike surface and indentations on the leaf margins; potato-leaf foliage has no indentations on the leaf margins.

TASTE is influenced by personal subjectivity and environmental conditions.

SEEDS indicates whether or not seeds are available commercially. Seeds for all varieties listed in this book are available to members of the Seed Savers Exchange.

Note: Some highly recommended varieties were not available for photographing. These varieties include Mirabell (thumb-size, pale yellow); Galina's (deep yellow cherry); Pruden's Purple, Jeff Davis, Stump of the World, and Fritz (pink beefsteaks); Dixie Golden Giant (yellow beefsteak); Azoychka (oblate yellow); Berwick German (bomb-shaped pink); Old Virginia, Diener, and St. Lucie (red beefsteaks); and Lillian's Red Kansas Paste (not really a paste type, small elongated ovals with a pointed tip).

AKER'S WEST VIRGINIA

Aker's West Virginia is a relatively new addition to my garden. It impressed me right away because it's a beautifully shaped plant—very symmetrical and relatively compact for an indeterminate variety. From germination until maturity, this is a vigorous grower with a prodigious yield. The stems at the base of the plant are exceptionally thick and sturdy. But attracted as I was by the plant's overall vigor, I was even more bowled over by the appearance and taste of the fruits.

The tomatoes grow in tight clusters, which is not common. At maturity, the deep red oblate fruits contrast beautifully with the dark green regular-leaf foliage. The taste of Aker's West Virginia is not lightweight; it packs a deep, robust flavor punch with a nice balance of flesh to juice. Usually about 10 ounces to a pound each, the tomatoes are almost universally blemish free, and they never show any cracking or blossom end rot.

This is one of many fantastic varieties from West Virginia, which has been the source for many heirloom tomatoes. There appears to be a strong seed-saving ethic in the state, especially in rural areas. Other heirloom varieties that hail from West Virginia include Tappy's Finest, Golden Ponderosa, Germaid Red, and West Virginia Straw.

TYPE: family
ORIGIN: United States
MATURITY: midseason
COLOR/SHAPE: deep red; oblate
SIZE/ARRANGEMENT: about 10 ounces to a pound, growing in clusters of two or three

YIELD: high
PLANT/FOLIAGE: indeterminate habit with heavy cover of regular-leaf foliage
TASTE: deep, robust, well-balanced
SEEDS: available commercially

Aker's West
Virginia

AMISH PASTE

Many people associate Amish or Mennonite farming with quality and taste, so the attraction to this variety is understandable given its name. In fact, the reason it ended up in my garden is because of its popularity among Seed Savers Exchange members. The yield is steady, and it never fails to produce reliably, bearing attractive 8- to 12-ounce fruits in clusters of two to four.

Despite the allure of this variety's name, I don't consider it to be a true paste tomato. By definition, a paste tomato usually has dry flesh and a low seed count. Amish Paste, however, is actually quite juicy and has an average amount of seeds. Another misconception has to do with its shape. Many growers describe it as heart-shaped, but it's really closer to a plum. The taste is somewhat mild and on the sweet side, and it doesn't linger long on the palate.

Amish Paste is a wimpy plant from start to finish—the narrow, dissected leaves just don't have much substance to them. Because the foliage is so sparse, the fruits are susceptible to sunscald late in the season. They're also prone to both concentric and radial cracking.

TYPE: family

ORIGIN: United States

MATURITY: midseason

COLOR/SHAPE: medium red elongated plums

SIZE/ARRANGEMENT: about 8 to 12 ounces, growing in clusters of two to four

YIELD: moderate to high

PLANT/FOLIAGE: indeterminate habit with sparse cover of narrow, regular-leaf foliage

Taste: mild, sweet

SEEDS: available commercially

Amish Paste

AMISH SALAD

This pink cherry tomato lasts forever on the vine. The abundant oval fruits literally just sit there looking at you for weeks without rotting. The flesh is very firm, almost hard, which contributes to its success among market gardeners. In this regard, Amish Salad is the exception to the general rule that heirloom tomatoes have softer flesh than their hybrid cousins. The taste of this variety won't wow you, but it's mild and pleasant. And the heavy production of fruits continues unabated throughout the summer.

Amish Salad is a huge plant with very heavy regular-leaf foliage cover, which is not typical of cherry tomatoes. It is remarkably tolerant of foliage diseases. What is typical of cherry tomatoes is that the fruits are universally blemish free, and are not susceptible to blossom end rot.

TYPE: family

ORIGIN: United States

MATURITY: midseason

COLOR/SHAPE: pink oval cherries

SIZE/ARRANGEMENT: about 2 ounces, growing in clusters of up to six

YIELD: very high, as with most cherries

PLANT/FOLIAGE: indeterminate habit with heavy cover of regular-leaf foliage

TASTE: mild, pleasant

SEEDS: not available commercially

Amish Salad

ANDREW RAHART'S JUMBO RED

While this tomato is not "jumbo" in size, it's huge in taste and aroma. The scent alone penetrates the senses, and is a mere hint of the outstanding taste to come. And that flavor is real tomato taste—not sweet or acidic, but deep and luscious. In fact, the flavor is so overwhelmingly good that it seduced me at first bite.

Andrew Rahart's Jumbo Red is a large, vigorous plant that supports a heavy yield of deep red beefsteak fruits, which are dense and weighty beyond their appearance. This variety is fairly tolerant of foliage diseases and has not shown blossom end rot. It has, however, exhibited some radial cracking in past years.

Andrew Rahart lived north of New York City and collected seeds from local immigrants in the area. Myona and Pink Ping Pong, a lovely large cherry tomato, are also attributed to him. The story behind the Myona name is especially interesting. When Mr. Rahart asked an Italian immigrant where he got the seeds, the man answered quite simply, "My own," but with his accent this was said "Myowna." Indeed, it was his own family heirloom from Italy.

TYPE: family

ORIGIN: unknown

MATURITY: late

COLOR/SHAPE: deep red beefsteaks

SIZE/ARRANGEMENT: about a pound, sometimes larger, singly or in pairs

YIELD: quite high for a large tomato

PLANT/FOLIAGE: indeterminate habit with medium to heavy cover of regular-leaf foliage

TASTE: rich, deep, luxurious, pure joy!

SEEDS: available commercially

Andrew Rahart's
Jumbo Red

ANNA RUSSIAN

Anna Russian is a truly gorgeous tomato—its fruit is shaped like the top of a Russian Orthodox church dome. As you can see from the cut tomato in the photograph, the long, heart-shaped fruits taper to a perfect point. The color can range from light pink to an almost red-pink, depending on the weather conditions from year to year.

Anna Russian is unique and unconventional in a number of ways. It has a sweet and juicy taste, which is usually not present in early tomatoes. It is the earliest-maturing heart-shaped tomato I know. Also, it's a heavy producer—not common for heart-shaped varieties—of 1-pound fruits in clusters of two or three.

Don't let the somewhat spindly growing plants and wispy, droopy foliage deter you from growing this terrific heirloom. Often growers become concerned, thinking that the plants are diseased, but many heart-shaped varieties have the same type of foliage. And although the foliage cover is medium to sparse, the fruits mature before sunscald becomes a problem.

TYPE: family

ORIGIN: Russia

MATURITY: early midseason

COLOR/SHAPE: pink hearts

SIZE/ARRANGEMENT: often in the 1-pound range, sometimes a bit smaller, growing in clusters of two or three

YIELD: usually high, which is remarkable for an early heart-shaped tomato

PLANT/FOLIAGE: indeterminate habit with sparse to medium cover of wispy, droopy regular-leaf foliage

TASTE: delicious, sweet, juicy

SEEDS: available commercially

Anna Russian

AUNT GINNY'S PURPLE

When newcomers to heirlooms first grow a tomato with "purple" in its name, they're often surprised that the color is not what they expect. In tomato language, the color purple translates as deep pink, with very few exceptions. This variety stands out because of its superior flavor and performance. It has an unforgettably rich and sweet taste. In fact, many growers have compared the flavor of Aunt Ginny's Purple to that of Pink Brandywine, which some consider the best-tasting heirloom available (and the yield of Aunt Ginny's Purple is superior to that of Pink Brandywine).

Aunt Ginny's Purple is a sizable plant with heavy potato-leaf foliage that is usually tolerant of most foliage diseases. While the fruits of some beefsteak varieties decline in size as the summer progresses, Aunt Ginny's Purple maintains its heft (1 pound plus) throughout the growing season. Some black stitching and radial cracking may appear under certain weather conditions, but I've seen no blossom end rot.

Often a person offering only one heirloom variety is overlooked by fellow Seed Savers Exchange members. Aunt Ginny's Purple came to me via a friend who had received it from a single listing. Had it not been discovered and given a glowing review in the Seed Savers Yearbook, this wonderful variety might not be around today.

TYPE: family

ORIGIN: Germany

MATURITY: late midseason

COLOR/SHAPE: deep pink beefsteaks

SIZE/ARRANGEMENT: usually in the 1-pound-plus range, growing in clusters of two or three

YIELD: moderate

PLANT/FOLIAGE: indeterminate habit with heavy cover of potato-leaf foliage

TASTE: luscious, on the sweet side, with complex undertones that linger

SEEDS: available commercially

*Aunt Ginny's
Purple*

AUNT RUBY'S GERMAN GREEN

Green tomatoes are particularly appealing because they have a spicy-sweet taste. In my opinion Aunt Ruby's German Green, Green, and Green Grape are the best examples of this unique flavor. But this wonderful taste can only be appreciated if the fruit is completely ripe, and that determination takes a bit of practice. (The cherry tomato Green Grape is easy in this regard because it has so many fruits that if you do pick an unripe one and find the flavor is not sweet and tangy, you'll still have lots of others to sample.)

Most green varieties form an amber blush on the blossom end when fully ripe. In addition to this, Aunt Ruby's German Green usually forms a pink blush on the blossom end that extends into the core. When the tomato is cut, you'll see a lovely mixture of neon green and pink. (The photo doesn't capture this pink blush, but it usually does appear.)

Aunt Ruby's German Green is the only true large green beefsteak I have ever seen. Most of the other green varieties are oblate and often mis-shapen. The heavy foliage cover of regular leaves is quite tolerant of disease. Occasionally, belly buttons and stitching may appear, but no blossom end rot has been seen by me.

What we observe as fruit color results from a combination of skin (epidermis) color and flesh color. Green flesh tomatoes don't lose all of their chlorophyll when they ripen. The flesh color will be a reddish-brown unless a specific gene is present; this gene inhibits formation of the red pigment (lycopene), resulting in a neon green color.

TYPE: family
ORIGIN: Germany
MATURITY: late
COLOR/SHAPE: green beefsteaks
SIZE/ARRANGEMENT: in the 1-pound range, growing in clusters of two or three

YIELD: usually moderate
PLANT/FOLIAGE: indeterminate habit with heavy cover of regular-leaf foliage
TASTE: spicy and sweet, scrumptious
SEEDS: available commercially

Aunt Ruby's German Green

BASINGA

There aren't many beefsteak heirloom tomatoes that maintain their true yellow color when ripe—most turn a deep gold color at maturity. Basinga is an exception, holding its light lemon-yellow coloration throughout its growing cycle.

There is a huge range of color among yellow tomatoes. All of them have a yellow epidermis, but there are variable amounts of beta carotene pigment in the flesh. The higher the beta carotene level in the flesh, the deeper the color, ranging from pale yellow to orange to deep golden yellow.

Basinga is the perfect tomato for those who crave a mild, sweet taste (although there have been reports that it develops a more intense flavor when grown in hotter climates like California). Many growers consider mild-tasting tomatoes to be low in acid. There are, however, no low-acid tomatoes—a high sugar content masks the acidity in varieties that many people think of as "low acid."

The plant is a variable producer of fruit, from moderate to heavy depending on the year. Basinga's regular-leaf foliage cover is sparse, which leaves the fruits susceptible to sunscald—cloth shading can prevent this condition. Some black stitching and belly buttons may occur, but the flavor is not affected by any surface blemishes.

TYPE: family

ORIGIN: unknown

MATURITY: midseason

COLOR/SHAPE: yellow beefsteaks

SIZE/ARRANGEMENT: about 6 ounces to 1 pound, growing in clusters of two or three

YIELD: usually high

PLANT/FOLIAGE: indeterminate habit with rather sparse cover of regular-leaf foliage

TASTE: pleasing, quite mild but not bland, somewhat sweet

SEEDS: not available commercially

Basinga

BIG RAINBOW

Heirloom tomato lovers often have mixed reactions to the gold-red bicolors such as Big Rainbow—some claim that they're tasteless, while others love the sweet, fruity flavor. In my experience, the flavor can vary markedly from variety to variety—and also within each variety—from year to year. But despite their unpredictable nature, I like Big Rainbow and other bicolors like Marizol Gold, Regina's Yellow, and Mary Robinson, which is the most highly colored bicolor I've grown (turning almost red at maturity).

The popularity of bicolors is due largely to the stunning color contrast of the flesh. The interior mottling of red and gold (as seen in the cut tomato in the photograph) is a visual delight. Newcomers to heirloom varieties are often enthralled by the unique color arrangement. All the gold-red heirloom bicolors have soft flesh, and don't keep for long.

Big Rainbow is a moderate producer of beefsteak tomatoes, and is typically a late-maturing plant. In fact, many varieties of bicolors are so late in maturing that they are grown more reliably in the South, but they do mature in my zone 5 garden. This tomato may also show concentric and longitudinal cracking under wet conditions.

It is believed that since so many of the gold-red bicolors have "German" in their name, or have been documented as coming from Germany, the original mutation that led to this class of tomatoes probably occurred in Germany or nearby.

TYPE: family
ORIGIN: unknown
MATURITY: late
COLOR/SHAPE: gold-red bicolor beefsteaks
SIZE/ARRANGEMENT: usually in the 1- to 2-pound range, growing singly or in pairs

YIELD: usually moderate
PLANT/FOLIAGE: indeterminate habit with heavy cover of regular-leaf foliage
TASTE: quite variable; fruity, sweet, and rich in a good year
SEEDS: available commercially

Big Rainbow

BLACK FROM TULA

Part of the fun and excitement of growing heirloom tomatoes is to experience the fantastic range of colors and tastes. First-time growers of black-type tomatoes are often astounded by the unique color. Some, unfortunately, are so put off by the unconventional appearance that they never get to truly enjoy the wonderful flavor.

There are those who claim that black tomatoes have a salty or even smoky flavor, but I've found them to be absolutely rich and sweet. When ripe, Black from Tula has prominent green shoulders and a dusky rose-black coloring. (When grown in the North, the black types don't develop the true blackish color that they do in the South.) The chocolate flesh is contrasted nicely with the deep green gel capsules that encase the seeds. The photograph also shows a distinctive spiral pattern of concentric cracking.

Black from Tula has a very heavy foliage cover of regular leaves, and is somewhat susceptible to early blight. The yield is moderate. It performs better for me than all the other black types except Noir de Crimée.

TYPE: family

ORIGIN: Ukraine

MATURITY: midseason

COLOR/SHAPE: smoky, dark reddish black with green shoulders; oblate

SIZE/ARRANGEMENT: about 10 to 12 ounces each, growing singly or in clusters of two or three

YIELD: moderate

PLANT/FOLIAGE: indeterminate habit with heavy cover of regular-leaf foliage

TASTE: rich and sweet

SEEDS: available commercially

Black
from Tula

BOX CAR WILLIE

B ox Car Willie was probably named after the legendary country singer. From seedling to mature plant, it's a fantastic performer. The vibrant red globes with orange undertones are visually stunning, and produce in abundance throughout the summer. In fact, the yield of Box Car Willie rivals or surpasses that of most hybrids. This makes it a good choice for market gardeners.

Box Car Willie has an outstanding, robust, old-fashioned tomato taste, and the fruits are extremely juicy. The heavy, dense cover of regular leaves has been relatively tolerant of foliage diseases, and I've never seen cracking or blossom end rot.

Box Car Willie belongs to a series of heirloom tomatoes created by the same person. Other varieties in the series include Lady Luck, Mule Team, Great Divide, Red Barn, and Pasture (a rampant red cherry variety that could be used to cover outhouse structures like the kudzu vine does in the South). I do prefer Box Car Willie and Mule Team to the others because of their superior yield and taste.

TYPE: created

ORIGIN: United States

MATURITY: midseason

COLOR/SHAPE: vibrant red with orange undertones; globular, sometimes oblate

SIZE/ARRANGEMENT: usually in the 1-pound range, some a bit smaller, growing in clusters of three or four

YIELD: very high

PLANT/FOLIAGE: indeterminate habit with heavy cover of regular-leaf foliage

TASTE: hearty, full-bodied, not sweet

SEEDS: available commercially

*Box Car
Willie*

BRANDYWINE, OTV

OTV Brandywine is one of four tomatoes that share the Brandywine name, so comparisons are inevitable. They're distinctive, however, with regard to fruit shape, color, taste, and foliage. OTV Brandywine originated from a natural cross-pollination between Yellow Brandywine and an unknown red parent. I dehybridized it for five years to an open-pollinated form. The "OTV" stands for *Off the Vine,* an heirloom tomato newsletter that Craig LeHoullier and I once published.

The beefsteak fruits of this variety are red with orange shoulders, and seldom have blemishes of any kind. (Many southern growers have noted that it does much better than Pink Brandywine in terms of setting fruit during high temperatures.) Among the Brandywine varieties, the yield of OTV Brandywine is second only to that of Red Brandywine. OTV Brandywine has a hefty taste that is not sweet, and the flesh is juicy yet meaty.

In my experience, potato-leaf varieties show exceptional tolerance of disease. This is likely because the leaf epidermis is thicker than that of regular-leaf foliage and forms a stronger barrier to infection. OTV Brandywine is typical in this regard, and rarely suffers from any foliage diseases.

TYPE: mystery

ORIGIN: United States

MATURITY: late midseason

COLOR/SHAPE: red beefsteaks with slightly orange shoulders

SIZE/ARRANGEMENT: usually in the 1-pound-plus range, growing in clusters of two or three

YIELD: moderate to high

PLANT/FOLIAGE: indeterminate habit with heavy cover of potato-leaf foliage

TASTE: rich, complex, not sweet

SEEDS: available commercially

Brandywine, OTV

BRANDYWINE, PINK

[SUDDUTH STRAIN]

Many adjectives have been used to describe the flavor of this wildly popular tomato—winey, robust, mouth-watering, sweet, tart, and complex. But until I grew the Sudduth strain of Pink Brandywine, I was not impressed. Other strains were just not exceptional in regard to taste, and they often produced malformed fruit.

All strains of Pink Brandywine have relatively low yields of fruit for two reasons. The first has to do with its malformed blossoms, which makes pollination difficult (although flicking the huge blossoms with your finger or shaking the plant can help). The second reason is not exclusive to this variety, but is rather a problem with all large-blossom potato-leaf plants. They simply don't pollinate well in areas of high, sustained heat.

Pink Brandywine is a brawny plant that produces fruits late in the growing season. The very deep pink beefsteaks reach 1 to 2 pounds in weight and have never shown blossom and rot. The potato-leaf foliage has been quite tolerant of foliage diseases.

Mrs. Sudduth, who gave seeds to the legendary tomato-seed collector Ben Quisenberry, claimed that the variety had been in her family for about a hundred years. Recent research suggests that Pink Brandywine was introduced through commercial seed firms. The origin of this tomato is unclear, but there is a precedent of commercial introductions originating from family heirlooms. Seedsman Alexander Livingston, for example, obtained a yellow tomato at a county fair and introduced it commercially in 1882 as Golden Queen.

TYPE: family

ORIGIN: United States

MATURITY: late

COLOR/SHAPE: deep pink beefsteaks

SIZE/ARRANGEMENT: usually in the 1- to 2-pound range, growing singly or in pairs

YIELD: low to moderate

PLANT/FOLIAGE: indeterminate habit with heavy cover of potato-leaf foliage

TASTE: winey, rich, complex

SEEDS: available commercially

Brandywine,
Pink

[Sudduth Strain]

BRANDYWINE, RED

Red Brandywine has been an outstanding performer in my garden for many years. It always yields a healthy number of perfect red globes. And because it consistently produces so many magnificent deep red fruits, it's an excellent heirloom for both the novice grower and the market gardener.

There's nothing subtle about Red Brandywine's taste—it explodes with flavor, literally assaulting your senses with every bite, and has a depth of flavor that truly matches its century-long heritage. The plant is tremendously vigorous and healthy, reliably producing 8- to 12-ounce fruits in clusters of four to six.

Very little historical information can be found about Red Brandywine in seed catalogs and Seed Savers Exchange sources. The variety is said to be named after the Brandywine River in eastern Pennsylvania.

TYPE: family

ORIGIN: United States

MATURITY: midseason

COLOR/SHAPE: perfect red globes

SIZE/ARRANGEMENT: usually in the 8- to 12-ounce range, occasionally to 1 pound, growing in clusters of four to six

YIELD: consistently high

PLANT/FOLIAGE: indeterminate habit with heavy cover of regular-leaf foliage

TASTE: intense, deep, rich, only slightly sweet

SEEDS: available commercially

Brandywine,
Red

BRANDYWINE, YELLOW

[PLATFOOT STRAIN]

The deep golden beefsteak fruits of Yellow Brandywine have a wonderfully complex and rich taste. The yield is prolific compared to that of Pink Brandywine, but not as abundant as that of Red Brandywine. Like the other Brandywines, this is a sturdy, vigorous plant and a solid performer in the garden.

Yellow Brandywine is one of the last varieties to ripen in my zone 5 garden, much later than the Pink or OTV Brandywines. Thus, it's important to get the plants transplanted to the garden in plenty of time for maturation before the first frost. Some fruits may have black stitching and clefts, but that hardly matters when the taste is so good. The potato-leaf foliage of this plant has been remarkably tolerant of foliage diseases.

I received this strain of Yellow Brandywine from Gary Platfoot of Ohio several years ago. The Platfoot strain offers a much higher yield than other strains, and the fruits have far fewer blemishes. Now, it's the only Yellow Brandywine I grow.

TYPE: family

ORIGIN: United States

MATURITY: late

COLOR/SHAPE: yellow beefsteaks, turning a deep gold

SIZE/ARRANGEMENT: mostly in the 1-pound range, growing singly or in clusters of two or three

YIELD: moderate

PLANT/FOLIAGE: indeterminate habit with heavy cover of potato-leaf foliage

TASTE: rich, complex, not sweet

SEEDS: available commercially

Brandywine, Yellow

[Platfoot Strain]

BREAK O' DAY

B reak O' Day is a workhorse of a tomato, reliably producing smooth, blemish-free fruits in abundance—it just won't let you down in any way. The scarlet red globe-shaped fruits are firmer than most. The taste is a true old-fashioned tomato flavor—somewhat tangy, with no sweetness.

The result of a cross between Marglobe and Marvana in 1923, Break O' Day is a genetically stabilized, open-pollinated selection that was introduced commercially in 1931. Some of the older open-pollinated varieties, including Break O' Day, really do produce at the same level as modern hybrids.

This variety is also excellent because of its resistance to cracking and blossom end rot, and its uniformity of fruit shape.

TYPE: commercial

ORIGIN: United States

MATURITY: midseason

COLOR/SHAPE: red globes

SIZE/ARRANGEMENT: about 8 to 12 ounces, growing in clusters of three or four

YIELD: usually high

PLANT/FOLIAGE: indeterminate habit with medium to heavy cover of regular-leaf foliage

TASTE: not sweet or bland, just a nice, old-fashioned tomato flavor

SEEDS: available commercially

Break O' Day

BRIANNA

Those interested in trying new heirloom varieties are often confronted with lists that have minimal descriptions. When that happens, many growers pick a variety simply because the name appeals to them. Sometimes, the names are quite colorful—like Duck Clucker, Turkey Chomp, and Stump of the World. Brianna was selected because its Celtic origins attracted me.

Brianna is a very large indeterminate plant with a heavy cover of potato-leaf foliage. The huge blossoms are the size of small marigolds (as are most of the pink-fruited potato-leaf varieties). This wouldn't be classified as a juicy tomato. The flesh is dense, with the sweet, rich flavor associated with most pink beefsteak heirlooms.

Many people have noted the similarity among pink-fruited potato-leaf varieties with respect to flavor, fruit shape, and foliage. The taste differences are so subtle that they simply have to be experienced. In fact, some heirloom tomato growers believe that over the years, many different names have been attached to a limited number of these varieties.

TYPE: family

ORIGIN: unknown

MATURITY: late midseason

COLOR/SHAPE: pink beefsteaks

SIZE/ARRANGEMENT: mostly in the 1-pound range, growing singly or in clusters of two or three

YIELD: moderate

PLANT/FOLIAGE: indeterminate habit with heavy cover of potato-leaf foliage

TASTE: sweet, rich, balanced

SEEDS: available commercially

Brianna

BULGARIAN #7

Bulgarian #7 has been exceptional with regard to taste and performance in only its first year in my garden. It was one of seven varieties given to me by tomato-history expert Andy Smith, whose son had recently spent a year in Bulgaria. The F1 hybrids were clearly marked as such (the #7 designation in the name refers to my numbering system), and most of those varieties were tough-skinned paste types, but this one was terrific.

The Bulgarian #7 plants I grew were just loaded with gorgeous crimson fruits that formed absolutely perfect globes until subjected to excessive rains, which resulted in some longitudinal cracking. The plant remains more compact than most indeterminate varieties. The yield was superb, and the foliage cover was excellent. Very little disease was seen during the one growing season, and no blossom end rot was evident.

Along with the general great performance of the plant, it was the taste of the fruits that convinced me to include Bulgarian #7 here. This tomato just exploded with juicy flavor after one bite. It was both tangy and sweet at the same time, and immediately impressed me as a potential new heirloom favorite.

TYPE: commercial

ORIGIN: Bulgaria

MATURITY: late midseason

COLOR/SHAPE: perfect red globes

SIZE/ARRANGEMENT: about 6 to 8 ounces, growing in clusters of three to six

YIELD: very high

PLANT/FOLIAGE: indeterminate habit with medium cover of regular-leaf foliage

TASTE: zippy yet sweet

SEEDS: not available commercially

Bulgarian #7

BULGARIAN TRIUMPH

In my experience, heirloom tomatoes with Bulgarian origins have superior flavor. Druzba, Bulgarian #7, and Bulgarian Triumph are all excellent varieties, each with unique and appealing traits. Bulgarian Triumph is similar to Bulgarian #7 in taste, while Druzba doesn't have the sweetness of the other two. Bulgarian Triumph has small fruits that are larger than typical cherry tomatoes, growing in clusters of four to six.

The fruits are always perfect, with never a blemish or blossom end rot. This tomato is very similar in appearance to the cluster-type tomatoes sold on the vine in some grocery stores. It has been a staple in my garden for many years.

Clusters of Bulgarian Triumph are extremely reliable in ripening evenly. Compared to the small size of the fruits, the taste, which is strong and sweet, really packs a wallop. This is a vigorous, sprawling medium-sized plant with a heavy leaf cover, and it can be susceptible to early blight.

TYPE: family

ORIGIN: Bulgaria

MATURITY: midseason

COLOR/SHAPE: red globes

SIZE/ARRANGEMENT: about 2 to 4 ounces, growing in clusters of four to six

YIELD: usually high

PLANT/FOLIAGE: indeterminate habit with medium to heavy cover of regular-leaf foliage

TASTE: strong and sweet, ambrosial

SEEDS: not available commercially

Bulgarian Triumph

CHEROKEE CHOCOLATE

Cherokee Chocolate was a spontaneous epidermal mutation of Cherokee Purple that appeared in Craig LeHoullier's garden a few years ago—the only difference between the two varieties is the skin color. Sometimes photographs don't adequately show the color differences between these two, but Cherokee Chocolate is a very distinctive mahogany brown. The taste differences, however, are negligible, but I've included this entry because it's an example of a spontaneous mutation). Spontaneous mutations are permanent, heritable traits that have been very important to the development of new tomato varieties with unique color combinations and tastes.

Cherokee Purple and Cherokee Chocolate are identical in terms of growth habit and fruit arrangement. The plants are very tolerant of foliage diseases and grow well in all zones. The photograph, taken after heavy rains, shows expanded concentric cracking in the fruit. The taste of both varieties fluctuates from year to year—fruits can be sweet and rich, or a bit watery and less flavorful. Devotees of Cherokee Chocolate, however, would not consider their garden complete without this tomato.

TYPE: family
ORIGIN: United States
MATURITY: midseason
COLOR/SHAPE: mahogany brown; oblate
SIZE/ARRANGEMENT: usually 6 to 12 ounces, sometimes to 1 pound, growing in clusters of two to four

YIELD: moderate to high
PLANT/FOLIAGE: indeterminate habit with heavy cover of regular-leaf foliage
TASTE: sweet, smoky, rich
SEEDS: not available commercially

Cherokee
Chocolate

CHEROKEE PURPLE

C herokee Purple and Cherokee Chocolate are essentially the same tomato, except for surface coloration. Both perform well in almost all climatic conditions and are relatively disease free. The color is unique, as is the taste, and the Cherokee-grown tradition is appealing to many heirloom aficionados.

Cherokee Purple is said to be more than 100 years old, originally grown by the Cherokee Indians (per J. D. Green, the original source). The variety quickly captured the fancy of catalog copy writers and its history has been expanded and embellished to a surprising degree. Such fanciful expansions of the known facts for Cherokee Purple—and countless other varieties—are a real concern to serious heirloom tomato growers.

TYPE: family

ORIGIN: United States

MATURITY: midseason

COLOR/SHAPE: dusty deep pink with purplish tint and green shoulders; oblate

SIZE/ARRANGEMENT: about 6 to 12 ounces or more, growing in clusters of two to four

YIELD: moderate to high

PLANT/FOLIAGE: indeterminate habit with heavy cover of regular-leaf foliage

TASTE: deep, rich, smoky, sweet

SEEDS: available commercially

Cherokee
Purple

CHRIS UKRAINIAN

hris Ukrainian, a fairly recent addition to my garden, has been a heavy producer of excellent-tasting tomatoes. It is one of the few varieties I grow that have both very large fruits and a high yield. It has also been disease tolerant in my garden, and no blossom end rot has been seen. If you grow many tomatoes from Ukraine, you already know that they're quite meaty and have similar, very sweet tastes.

Chris Ukrainian is a light pink beefsteak variety with a moderate foliage cover of regular leaves. It is a very firm tomato, and the flesh is dense and not particularly juicy.

TYPE: family

ORIGIN: Ukraine

MATURITY: late midseason

COLOR/SHAPE: light pink beefsteaks, occasionally with green shoulders

SIZE/ARRANGEMENT: often in the 1- to 2-pound range, a few smaller, growing in clusters of two to four

YIELD: exceptionally high for such a large tomato

PLANT/FOLIAGE: indeterminate habit with medium cover of regular-leaf foliage

TASTE: nice balanced flavor, with sweetness

SEEDS: not available commercially

Chris Ukrainian

CRNKOVIC YUGOSLAVIAN

C rnkovic Yugoslavian has a superb, rich taste with a pronounced sweetness. Year after year it has performed well with relatively good tolerance of foliage diseases. Unlike almost all other large pink beefsteaks, it usually has a high yield. Occasionally, low temperatures at pollination time result in fruits that have some clefts (as shown in this photograph), but this doesn't happen every year.

Yasha Crnkovic (pronounced KRINK-o-vitch), a colleague of mine, obtained some heirloom tomato varieties for me from relatives in Yugoslavia. This one was the very best (another good one in the group, Yasha Yugoslavian, bears large pink, heart-shaped fruits).

TYPE: family

ORIGIN: Yugoslavia

MATURITY: midseason

COLOR/SHAPE: pink beefsteaks

SIZE/ARRANGEMENT: usually 1 to 2 pounds, growing in clusters of two or three

YIELD: high for such a large tomato

PLANT/FOLIAGE: indeterminate habit with medium cover of regular-leaf foliage

TASTE: very deep, rich and sweet

SEEDS: available commercially

Crnkovic
Yugoslavian

CUOSTRALÉE

Along with Omar's Lebanese and Zogola, Cuostralée is an excellent tomato for those who are interested in growing the biggest fruits possible. They can reach up to 3 pounds in size if grown under ideal conditions (some of my tomatoes were so heavy that they fell off the vine during preparation for photography). But in addition to its size, Cuostralée has superb taste and yield, which is not at all common for a tomato this large. The flavor is intense and pure—neither tart nor sweet, but well-balanced.

The plant itself is huge and often dwarfs nearby varieties. Some tomatoes are very sensitive to environmental changes, and taste and fruit size are the usual victims when inclement weather arrives, but Cuostralée has been absolutely consistent year after in terms of productivity and flavor. It is somewhat susceptible to foliage diseases.

A spontaneous skin mutation of this tomato appeared in my garden years ago. Yellow skin makes a red-fleshed tomato appear red, and the mutation was to clear skin, which made the tomato pink. Both strains are identical, except for skin color.

This variety came from Norbert Parreira of Hellimer, France, who had offered to trade seeds with some Seed Savers Exchange members.

TYPE: family

ORIGIN: France

MATURITY: late midseason

COLOR/SHAPE: red beefsteaks with some ribbing at the shoulders

SIZE/ARRANGEMENT: almost always over 1 pound, with many in the 2- to 3-pound range, growing in clusters of two or three

YIELD: very high

PLANT/FOLIAGE: indeterminate habit with medium cover of regular-leaf foliage

TASTE: strong, intense, classic tomato flavor

SEEDS: available commercially

Cuostralée

DEBBIE

Many of the best heirloom tomatoes are pink, fewer are red, and still fewer have that orange undertone that we associate with modern hybrids. Debbie is one of the few good red-orange heirlooms, along with OTV Brandywine and Break O' Day. It is known for its performance, which can be described as extremely consistent.

The taste is tart and zippy, not sweet, and the flesh is dense and heavy, but not juicy. The plant's heavy cover of regular leaves is very tolerant of foliage diseases. Debbie's yield is variable, depending on the weather.

I almost overlooked this variety when making selections for this book, but my closest tomato colleagues reminded me to consider Debbie for inclusion because it's simply a delight to grow.

TYPE: family

ORIGIN: Poland

MATURITY: late midseason

COLOR/SHAPE: red beefsteaks with orange shoulders and undertones

SIZE/ARRANGEMENT: mostly in the 12-ounce to 1-pound range, growing in tight clusters of two or three

YIELD: moderate to high

PLANT/FOLIAGE: indeterminate habit with heavy cover of regular-leaf foliage

TASTE: rich, robust, zesty

SEEDS: not available commercially

Debbie

DR. CAROLYN

several years ago, saved seeds from Galina's, which is a deep yellow cherry tomato with potato-leaf foliage from Siberia, gave rise to an amazing array of different-colored cherry tomatoes. Instead of the expected yellow fruits, the tomatoes were red, salmon, pink, and ivory. Since they remained cherry-shaped, I knew the results were not due to either accidental cross-pollination or a spontaneous mutation. The most reasonable explanation was that Galina's could sometimes exhibit genetic instability.

Steve Draper, a tomato friend who had also found Galina's to be somewhat genetically unstable, grew out my seeds for the various colored cherries, and only the ivory variant had the superb flavor of the original Galina's. Steve then introduced it to the Seed Savers Exchange, and to my surprise, he named it Dr. Carolyn.

Dr. Carolyn is a huge, vigorous plant with a medium cover of regular-leaf foliage that is quite resistant to disease. The fruits range from pale ivory to deep yellow, depending on the weather and degree of foliage cover (the heavier the canopy, the lighter the color of the tomatoes). This variety retains a taste character similar to that of Galina's—a burst of flavor that has true depth, unlike most cherry tomatoes.

TYPE: mystery

ORIGIN: United States

MATURITY: early midseason

COLOR/SHAPE: pale ivory to yellow cherries

SIZE/ARRANGEMENT: about 1 ounce, growing in clusters of eight

YIELD: very high

PLANT/FOLIAGE: indeterminate habit with medium cover of regular-leaf foliage

TASTE: strong bursts of flavor, with a nice balance of sweet and tart

SEEDS: available commercially

Dr. Carolyn

DR. LYLE

D r. Lyle is a distinctive tomato in a number of ways. It is one of only a few varieties that have white to pale ivory blossoms, and its gray-green regular-leaf foliage is also unique (some tomato varieties have a novelty Angora-type foliage, which is gray-green and fuzzy to the touch, but Dr. Lyle is the only one with this coloring plus regular leaves).

Dr. Lyle is a sizeable plant that loads up with large, deep pink beefsteaks. The foliage cover is heavy, so be sure to check at the base of the plant for developing fruits, especially if you let them sprawl—it's easy to miss ripe tomatoes.

The fruits of Dr. Lyle are absolutely voluptuous, but it's the taste that makes this variety outstanding—the rich, complex flavors run broad and deep. The yield is uniformly high, and the plant has exhibited excellent tolerance of foliage diseases.

The growth habit and leaf shape suggest that this is one of the older heirlooms, but unfortunately, the identity of Dr. Lyle remains a mystery.

TYPE: family

ORIGIN: United States

MATURITY: late

COLOR/SHAPE: deep pink beefsteaks

SIZE/ARRANGEMENT: mostly in the 1- to 2-pound range, growing in clusters of two or three

YIELD: consistently high

PLANT/FOLIAGE: indeterminate habit with heavy cover of regular-leaf foliage

TASTE: deep, intensely rich, sweet

SEEDS: available commercially

Dr. Lyle

DR. NEAL

The huge plants of Dr. Neal are consistently loaded with meaty, super-tasting beefsteak tomatoes. The heavy cover of regular-leaf foliage is quite tolerant of foliage diseases (be sure to check the interior of the plants, as ripened fruits may be hidden underneath). It's important to allow the tomatoes to fully ripen on the vine in order to appreciate their superb flavor. In some years Dr. Neal produces very light pink tomatoes, and in other years the fruits are a very deep pink (pigment production is influenced by environmental conditions). Regardless of the color, though, these beefsteaks are very dense, with a rich tomato taste that's sweeter in some years than in others.

Note the one very malformed fruit in the photograph. This condition is called catfacing, and it happens when pollination occurs at low temperatures. Although such fruits won't win a beauty contest, they're just fine to eat.

Very little is known about the origin of Dr. Neal, but finely dissected leaves like these usually indicate that the variety is an old one.

TYPE: commercial

ORIGIN: United States

MATURITY: late

COLOR/SHAPE: pink beefsteaks

SIZE/ARRANGEMENT: mostly in the 1-pound-plus range, growing in clusters of two or three

YIELD: moderate

PLANT/FOLIAGE: indeterminate habit with heavy cover of regular-leaf foliage

TASTE: rich, strong, assertive

SEEDS: available commercially

Dr. Neal

DR. WYCHE'S YELLOW

Many people think the lighter-colored yellow tomatoes are bland—and indeed some are—but Dr. Wyche's Yellow is not one of them. Its deep and rich taste can compete with the best of the red and pink varieties. The fruits are meaty, dense, and usually blemish free. The flesh is almost porous because of the numerous seed chambers.

Dr. Wyche's color is typical of most yellow varieties in turning a deep gold at maturity. Despite the sparse foliage cover, which can lead to sunscald, this tomato ranks as one of the best yellow beefsteaks available.

There was a Dr. Wyche, but very little about him is known other than that he lived on a mountainside not too far from a zoo. His gardens were liberally fertilized with manure from the zoo, and were reported to be quite lush.

TYPE: family

ORIGIN: United States

MATURITY: late midseason

COLOR/SHAPE: deep golden beefsteaks

SIZE/ARRANGEMENT: mostly in the 1-pound range, growing in clusters of two to four

YIELD: moderate

PLANT/FOLIAGE: indeterminate habit with sparse cover of regular-leaf foliage

TASTE: rich, complex, not bland

SEEDS: available commercially

Dr. Wyche's
Yellow

DRUZBA

D ruzba is a virtually problem-free garden performer. It is widely adapted for growth in almost all parts of the United States, has a high yield, and is tolerant of foliage diseases. The deep red globes are blemish free and pack a robust taste. The flavor doesn't overpower you with sweetness but is exquisitely balanced, and the flesh has a nice blend of juice and meat. Heavy rains caused some longitudinal cracking in the fruits, but most varieties suffer the same fate in wet conditions.

Druzba is ideal for nearly every type of gardener and deserves recognition as one of the finest heirlooms available. Novice gardeners will find it a breeze to grow, market gardeners will appreciate the high yield and uniformly blemish-free fruits, and organic gardeners will love its tolerance of disease. This is truly a tomato for the masses.

Norbert Parreira of Hellimer, France, who provided the seeds, identified them as Bulgarian in origin. Alternate spellings of this variety name are Drushba and Druzhba (the word *druzhba* means "friendship" in Bulgarian). The USDA listed this variety as Drushba, and it was identical to the variety from Mr. Parreira. There is a town called Druzhba in Ukraine, but my source clearly indicated a Bulgarian origin.

TYPE: family

ORIGIN: Bulgaria

MATURITY: late midseason

COLOR/SHAPE: deep red globes

SIZE/ARRANGEMENT: 8 ounces to 1 pound, growing in clusters of three to five

YIELD: very high

PLANT/FOLIAGE: indeterminate habit with heavy cover of regular-leaf foliage

TASTE: authoritative but balanced, just superb

SEEDS: available commercially, as Druzba, Drushba, or Druzhba

Druzba

EARL OF EDGECOMBE

The history of this tomato dates back to when the sixth earl of Edgecombe died. His nearest living relative resided in New Zealand on a sheep farm, and when he returned to England to claim the title of seventh earl of Edgecombe, he brought this tomato variety with him. The seeds were sent to me by Ulrike Paradine of England, who obtained them from the Henry Doubleday Research Association, a British organization with functions similar to the Seed Savers Exchange in terms of preserving heirloom varieties.

Orange tomatoes can be either too bland or too strong in taste, but varieties like Earl of Edgecombe, Orange Strawberry, and Kellogg's Breakfast are the exceptions. Earl of Edgecombe has a very pronounced, robust flavor and is very meaty, with fewer seeds than normal fruits.

Earl of Edgecombe is a favorite because of its superb flavor, high yield, and uniform, blemish-free fruits that have never shown cracking of any kind in my garden. The foliage appears to be quite tolerant of disease, but I have seen blossom end rot on some of the earliest fruits (it disappears, however, as the season progresses). The very deep, almost glowing orange color is visually exciting.

TYPE: family

ORIGIN: New Zealand

MATURITY: late midseason

COLOR/SHAPE: deep orange globes

SIZE/ARRANGEMENT: usually 6 to 10 ounces, growing in clusters of three to five

YIELD: high

PLANT/FOLIAGE: indeterminate but compact habit with heavy cover of regular-leaf foliage

TASTE: rich, sweet, and tart all at one time

SEEDS: available commercially

Earl of Edgecombe

EVA PURPLE BALL

S eed Savers Exchange members, personal experience, and anecdotes from others have convinced me that there are no obvious faults with this outstanding variety. Eva Purple Ball is widely adapted and seems to perform well for everyone, everywhere. Many growers gush over the absolutely perfect pink globes, but if you look closely, you can see that the surface has a fine mottling of white. I've seen that mottling on only one other variety, Redfield Beauty. The only fault it has is that ripe fruits tend to drop spontaneously from the vine. The taste is lauded by all who grow it as being sweet, luscious, and quite juicy.

What impresses most about this tomato is its ability to reliably produce perfect, uniform globes year after year. Despite weather variables, the yield is high. The plant shows excellent tolerance of foliage diseases, and I've never seen blossom end rot develop.

Seeds were originally brought from the Black Forest region of Germany in the late 1800s. Like varieties with Amish or Mennonite backgrounds, tomatoes from this area hold a certain charm to heirloom aficionados.

TYPE: family

ORIGIN: Germany

MATURITY: midseason

COLOR/SHAPE: perfect pink globes with a fine white mottling

SIZE/ARRANGEMENT: about 6 to 8 ounces, growing in clusters of three to five

YIELD: high

PLANT/FOLIAGE: indeterminate habit with medium cover of regular-leaf foliage

TASTE: sweet, absolutely delicious

SEEDS: available commercially

*Eva Purple
Ball*

GERMAID RED

E very so often, a truly outstanding variety is not grown because it's difficult to obtain the seeds. This was the case with Germaid Red until its recent commercial introduction. This tomato has a truly intense, old-fashioned taste. Although the photograph suggests a heart shape, the fruits are really elongated beefsteaks with no clear point at the blossom end like a true heart. The color is a deep red, the flesh is quite dense, and there is distinct ribbing at the shoulders.

Germaid Red is a very healthy and stout plant with a dense cover of regular-leaf foliage. The yield is variable from year to year, but usually it's very high for a beefsteak.

TYPE: family

ORIGIN: United States

MATURITY: late midseason

COLOR/SHAPE: deep red elongated beefsteaks with ribbing at the shoulders

SIZE/ARRANGEMENT: mostly in the 1-pound range, growing in clusters of three to five

YIELD: usually on the high side

PLANT/FOLIAGE: indeterminate habit with heavy cover of regular-leaf foliage

TASTE: wonderful, rich, not sweet

SEEDS: available commercially

Germaid Red

GERMAN HEAD

S eeds of German Head have been commercially available for a long time, but curiously, it's seldom mentioned as an outstanding heirloom variety. The exquisite, rich flavor of this dark pink beefsteak made me a convert for life—it's that good. The texture of the flesh is noteworthy for being very creamy. The only other varieties with a similar wonderful texture are Lillian's Yellow Heirloom and Jeff Davis.

Plants are very sturdy, with excellent foliage cover and little foliage disease. The consistent high yield and blemish-free fruits also make it a good choice, especially for market gardeners.

Gleckler's Seed Company in Metamora, Ohio, one of the first firms in the United States to offer heirloom tomato seeds for sale, originally listed this variety. Their catalog was a delight because it included so many hard-to-get vegetables, but unfortunately they went out of business a few years ago.

TYPE: family

ORIGIN: Germany

MATURITY: late midseason

COLOR/SHAPE: dark pink beefsteaks

SIZE/ARRANGEMENT: mostly in the 12-ounce to 1-pound range, growing in clusters of two or three

YIELD: very high

PLANT/FOLIAGE: indeterminate habit with heavy cover of regular-leaf foliage

TASTE: just exquisite, smooth, luscious, not especially sweet

SEEDS: available commercially

German Head

GERMAN RED STRAWBERRY

G erman Red Strawberry is easily one of the best-tasting tomatoes I've ever grown. The aroma is enchanting, providing a delightful preview of the pleasures to come. The exquisitely rich, complex flavor develops on the palate with undertones of slight sweetness that linger.

The name "strawberry" is appropriate in this variety because the points of the heart-shaped fruits are blunted like strawberries. The photograph doesn't do it justice since the plants were not at their prime when shooting took place. The fruit at the bottom also shows catfacing due to cold conditions prevalent in late June and July. Fruit shape can be variable depending on the weather, but later-maturing fruits are almost always true to the aforementioned strawberry shape.

Although the seedlings and early transplants of German Red Strawberry look somewhat spindly, they grow into nice sturdy plants in the garden. In addition, the yield of this variety is better than that of most heart-shaped tomatoes.

TYPE: family

ORIGIN: Germany

MATURITY: late

COLOR/SHAPE: red fruits of variable shape, with later-maturing fruits almost always strawberry-shaped

SIZE/ARRANGEMENT: mostly in the 1-pound-plus range, growing in clusters of two or three

YIELD: high for a heart-shaped tomato

PLANT/FOLIAGE: indeterminate habit with medium cover of regular-leaf foliage

TASTE: superior, complex, slightly sweet

SEEDS: available commercially

German Red
Strawberry

GOGOSHA

ogosha is the lightest pink beefsteak I've ever seen—the color can accurately be described as cotton-candy pink. Its wonderful taste is typical of pink beefsteaks from the Ukraine in being sweet, rich, and absolutely juicy.

This variety develops a heavy canopy of potato-leaf foliage that is especially tolerant of diseases. The yield is generally good, and fruits are a pound and more, growing in clusters of two or three.

This heirloom was given to me by a student, Tanya Gogosha, who said it came from the Tarnipal region of Ukraine and was brought to America in the late 1800s by her family.

TYPE: family

ORIGIN: Ukraine

MATURITY: late midseason

COLOR/SHAPE: lightest pink beefsteaks

SIZE/ARRANGEMENT: in the 1-pound-plus range, growing in clusters of two or three

YIELD: moderate

PLANT/FOLIAGE: indeterminate habit with heavy cover of potato-leaf foliage

TASTE: sweet, mouthwatering

SEEDS: available commercially

Gogosha

GOLD BALL, LIVINGSTON'S

The proper name for this tomato is Livingston's Gold Ball, to reflect the fact that it was introduced by the Livingston Seed Company in 1892. The variety Golden Queen, on the other hand, also introduced by Livingston (and which follows this entry), is almost never listed as Livingston's Golden Queen. Gold Ball is thought to be an improvement on Green Gage, a small yellow-fruited pre-1800 variety. However, if you compare the photographs of the two in this book, you'll see that the fruit size, shape, and clustering of the two varieties are quite different.

Even if you usually prefer tomatoes that are a bit sweet, Gold Ball may appeal to you. Many tomatoes introduced commercially in the late 1800s had a certain flavor, more robust than sweet, just not found in later commercial introductions. Gold Ball is a good example of this taste. The plant's yield is high and disease tolerance is excellent. The fruits are larger than cherry tomatoes but are still quite small (2 to 3 ounces) when compared to the typical small tomato of 4 to 6 ounces.

TYPE: commercial
ORIGIN: United States
MATURITY: midseason
COLOR/SHAPE: golden globes
SIZE/ARRANGEMENT: about 2 to 3 ounces, growing in clusters of six to eight

YIELD: very high
PLANT/FOLIAGE: indeterminate habit with heavy cover of regular-leaf foliage
TASTE: not shy, more on the zingy side than sweet
SEEDS: not available commercially

Gold Ball, Livingston's

GOLDEN QUEEN
[USDA STRAIN]

Golden Queen was originally described by seedsman Alexander Livingston in the late 1800s as having a very distinctive pink, pearly blush that starts at the blossom end and moves up toward the stem end. This characteristic, however, is not present in most current commercial offerings of Golden Queen. It was not until I grew out a strain of Golden Queen obtained from the USDA seed bank that I found a variety to match the original description. And while many white and yellow varieties are known to show a pink tinge at the blossom end, this strain exhibits a very intense pink coloration that also extends upward toward the stem end.

The USDA strain of Golden Queen tastes better than other Golden Queen strains now in commerce. This rich, complex flavor is not often found in yellow tomatoes, which tend to be bland. In addition, the variety is very productive and the foliage is quite tolerant of disease.

Golden Queen is clearly documented as being a family heirloom that was discovered by Alexander Livingston at a county fair. He later selected for and improved the strain, then released it commercially as Golden Queen in 1882. This method of acquiring family heirlooms, improving on them, and releasing them commercially was probably common, but seldom has there been such clear substantiation as we have for Golden Queen.

TYPE: family

ORIGIN: United States

MATURITY: midseason

COLOR/SHAPE: deep golden with a pink, pearly blush at maturity; oblate

SIZE/ARRANGEMENT: about 8 to 12 ounces, growing in clusters of three to five

YIELD: moderate to high

PLANT/FOLIAGE: indeterminate habit with medium cover of regular-leaf foliage

TASTE: deep, rich, just lovely

SEEDS: USDA strain not available commercially

*Golden
Queen*
[USDA Strain]

GREEN

Despite this tomato's obviously straightforward name, it's sometimes called Dorothy's Green, after the woman who first introduced it to the Seed Savers Exchange. Some folks describe it as having stripes, but as you can see from the large beefsteak in the center, it really isn't striped in the true sense. The photograph is very helpful in showing the amber color that must develop to indicate ripeness, and the lovely interior neon green of the flesh is also shown well.

This variety is almost as good as Aunt Ruby's German Green in regard to taste and performance. It has the special flavor I look for in green-when-ripe types—a luscious, spicy sweetness. This is not a particularly vigorous plant, with its sparse to medium foliage cover of regular leaves. The shape of the fruits can be slightly variable—some are oblate while others are beefsteak.

Of the green varieties I have grown, this one, Aunt Ruby's German Green, and Evergreen have been most reliable in producing fruits that are not malformed. Other green varieties tend to exhibit clefts and blemishes, and are oddly shaped.

TYPE: family

ORIGIN: United States

MATURITY: midseason

COLOR/SHAPE: green with an amber color at the blossom end when ripe; variable shape, with some beefsteaks, others oblate

SIZE/ARRANGEMENT: mostly in the 6- to 12-ounce range, with some larger, growing in clusters of three or four

YIELD: moderate

PLANT/FOLIAGE: indeterminate habit with sparse to medium cover of regular-leaf foliage

TASTE: wonderful spicy sweetness

SEEDS: available commercially, as Green or Dorothy's Green

Green

GREEN GAGE

This tomato was found in the USDA seed collection, and most sources suggest it is a pre-1800 variety. Some say it's called Green Gage after the plum of the same name (although Green Gage plums are green, not yellow, the shape is pretty close). Others have speculated that the green in the name refers to the green color of the gel capsules that surround each seed until the tomato is ripe. If you eat the fruits before the gel capsules turn yellow, it doesn't taste very good. But once this variety is fully ripe—indicated by a uniform yellow color and presence of yellow (not green) gel capsules around the seeds—you'll have a hint of what a tomato tasted like two hundred years ago.

Green Gage has a strong, tangy flavor. The fruits are bright yellow at maturity, and have a slightly elongated globe shape. This is a hearty plant with a very heavy regular-leaf foliage cover. Green Gage also has a prolific yield.

Most memorable to me about growing Green Gage was the sole branch that developed only red fruits during one growing season a few years ago. That is called a "somatic mutation," and it's the same as what is referred to as a "bud sport" in fruit trees. The red tomatoes on that branch were identical in size and shape to the yellow fruits. Recently, I read that Green Gage existed as both a red and a yellow variety, which indicates that the somatic mutation in my garden may not be that unusual.

TYPE: family

ORIGIN: Europe

MATURITY: midseason

COLOR/SHAPE: bright yellow, slightly elongated globes

SIZE/ARRANGEMENT: larger than cherries, about 2 to 3 ounces, growing in clusters of five or six

YIELD: high

PLANT/FOLIAGE: indeterminate habit with heavy cover of regular-leaf foliage

TASTE: intense, zesty, snappy

SEEDS: not available commercially

Green Gage

GREEN GRAPE

First-time growers of Green Grape have a tendency to fall in love with it after only one season. Because of the wide availability of seeds, it is usually the first green-when-ripe type most people grow. And when you experience the unique spicy sweetness associated with green tomatoes for the first time, it's easy to become addicted. Many people also like to grow different-colored cherry tomatoes, and Green Grape is the only true green cherry tomato available.

The heavy foliage cover of regular leaves on this huge and rangey plant is excellent, and it's very tolerant of foliage diseases. As is the case with most cherry tomatoes, the yield is always very high, although the fruits do have a tendency to split during wet conditions.

It takes some practice to determine when a green tomato is ripe. There will usually be an amber blush on the blossom end of the fruit that extends up toward the stem end. There is a range of color within each cluster, and the ripest ones, which are yellowish amber, are nearest the main stem. If they aren't fully ripe, they taste sour, so practice makes perfect because the fully ripe tomato flavor is a sensational reward.

TYPE: created

ORIGIN: United States

MATURITY: midseason

COLOR/SHAPE: green cherries turning amber when ripe

SIZE/ARRANGEMENT: about 1 ounce, growing in clusters of six to eight

YIELD: usually high

PLANT/FOLIAGE: indeterminate habit with heavy cover of regular-leaf foliage

TASTE: spicy, sweet, outstanding

SEEDS: available commercially

Green Grape

GREEN ZEBRA

Green Zebra is one of the most visually enchanting tomatoes available. When young, it has dark green stripes set against a light green background; at maturity, a lighter green striping appears against a yellow-amber background. The flesh of this novelty tomato is neon green, similar to that of green types like Aunt Ruby's German Green. Green Zebra has clustered fruits that are slightly bigger than a ping-pong ball.

Alice Waters of Chez Panisse in California is said to have made this variety popular because of its coloration and taste, which has been described as sweet and tangy at the same time. I have found the flavor to be a bit on the astringent side.

The foliage is not heavy, but the plants are nonetheless vigorous and show excellent disease tolerance. Blemish-free fruits are produced in abundance.

Green Zebra, along with the variety Tigerella, a red tomato with jagged gold stripes, will elicit audible delight from newcomers to heirloom tomatoes.

TYPE: created

ORIGIN: United States

MATURITY: midseason

COLOR/SHAPE: yellowish green with stripes; oblate

SIZE/ARRANGEMENT: larger than cherries, about 2 to 3 ounces, growing in clusters of three to five

YIELD: moderate

PLANT/FOLIAGE: indeterminate but compact habit with medium cover of regular-leaf foliage

TASTE: zippy, slightly astringent, although many detect sweet overtones

SEEDS: available commercially

Green Zebra

GROSSE COTELÉE

Most pink tomatoes are known for their sweet, rich taste, and Grosse Cotelée is no exception. It has a nice balanced flavor that's equal parts tart and sweet, and memorable for lingering in your mouth. Grosse Cotelée will occasionally exhibit ribbing at the shoulders, which makes the fruits especially attractive. This characteristic, however, is variable.

Although this variety is indeterminate, the sturdy plant stays quite compact. Disease tolerance of the heavy regular-leaf foliage has been consistently excellent over the years. The yield of largely blemish-free fruits has been high, but this can change, depending on the weather from year to year. Concentric cracking and blossom end rot have been present at times.

TYPE: family

ORIGIN: France

MATURITY: late

COLOR/SHAPE: pink; oblate

SIZE/ARRANGEMENT: mostly in the 8- to 12-ounce range, growing in clusters of three or four

YIELD: moderate to high

PLANT/FOLIAGE: indeterminate but compact habit with heavy cover of regular-leaf foliage

TASTE: full, balanced, with winey undertones

SEEDS: available commercially

Grosse
Cotelée

HEIDI

Many paste tomatoes have weak flavor—overall, they're just bland. Heidi is an exception in that it has a true tomato taste. The flavors are sweet and mild, but rich.

For the paste-happy gardener, Heidi is ideal. The fruits are very dense but have few tomato seeds (a big letdown for seed savers). The walls are thick, but the skin is not tough. The yield is very high, and the fruits last well on the vine.

Most heirloom and hybrid paste tomatoes are known for susceptibility to both blossom end rot and early blight. Heidi bucks this trend. In fact, unless the garden is almost under water, it faithfully seems to resist blossom end rot. And Heidi has also been remarkably tolerant of all foliage diseases in my zone 5 garden. This plant is what I'd call semi-determinate; it's more compact than an indeterminate plant.

The origin of Heidi is West African, which is quite rare. The seeds came to me from Heidi Iyok, a student of mine from Cameroon.

TYPE: family

ORIGIN: Cameroon

MATURITY: midseason

COLOR/SHAPE: red pears

SIZE/ARRANGEMENT: about 4 ounces, growing in clusters of four or five

YIELD: high

PLANT/FOLIAGE: semi-determinate habit with heavy cover of regular-leaf foliage

TASTE: sweet, mild but not bland

SEEDS: not available commercially

Heidi

HERMAN'S YELLOW

Contrary to its name, Herman's Yellow is actually a deep golden-orange. It is one of the two best-tasting yellow-golden-orange hearts available (the other being Orange Strawberry). For me the taste of Orange Strawberry is slightly better, but Herman's Yellow is still an impressive heart-shaped specimen.

These beauties have a fine-grained flesh that can be described as almost creamy. The fruits are perfectly formed and seldom have blemishes. Herman's Yellow also has exceptional taste—a complex, rich, sometimes fruity flavor.

This variety appears spindly throughout the seedling and transplant stages, but grows very well once established in the garden. Herman's Yellow features the wispy, droopy leaves found in so many heart-shaped varieties, which is perfectly normal and doesn't indicate disease. Because the foliage can be sparse, the only complaint with this tomato is its susceptibility to sunscald.

TYPE: family

ORIGIN: United States

MATURITY: late

COLOR/SHAPE: gold-orange hearts

SIZE/ARRANGEMENT: mostly 12 ounces to 1 pound or more, growing in clusters of two or three

YIELD: moderate

PLANT/FOLIAGE: indeterminate habit with sparse to medium cover of finely dissected, regular-leaf foliage

TASTE: intense but balanced, with hints of citrus

SEEDS: not available commercially

Herman's Yellow

HUGH'S

Hugh's has a large following among Seed Savers Exchange members, and with good reason. The main attraction is the outstanding sweet yet complex flavor. In fact, it's worth growing not only for its superb taste, but also because it produces very heavy yields for such a large-fruited variety. Along with Lillian's Yellow Heirloom and Basinga, Hugh's is unique in retaining a clear pale yellow color at maturity. The flesh is very soft, and consequently the fruits don't last very long on the vine. All three varieties have superb taste (I think Lillian's has the slightly better flavor and flesh texture, but Hugh's and Basinga have superior yields.)

Although the plant appears fragile in the early stages, it thrives after transplanting out, growing into a sizable plant. Hugh's has been susceptible to early blight in my garden, and the sparse foliage cover of regular leaves does make it more prone to sunscald.

Jeff McCormack, of the Southern Exposure Seed Exchange, claims that this variety is from Madison County, Indiana, and dates back to 1940.

TYPE: family

ORIGIN: United States

MATURITY: late

COLOR/SHAPE: pale yellow beefsteaks

SIZE/ARRANGEMENT: usually 1 to 2 pounds, growing in pairs

YIELD: moderate to high

PLANT/FOLIAGE: indeterminate habit with sparse to medium cover of regular-leaf foliage

TASTE: strong, delightful, with a pronounced sweetness

SEEDS: available commercially

Hugh's

HUNGARIAN OVAL

Hungarian Oval is one of only a handful of tomatoes that I consider very dense: in relation to its size, the weight is noticeable the first time you hold one in your hand. The other hefty varieties are German Red Strawberry, Andrew Rahart's Jumbo Red, Zogola, and Russian #117.

Hungarian Oval has a very meaty consistency and few seeds. The taste is intense and exuberant with great depth, and the aroma of the cut flesh is earthy and enticing. The foliage cover of regular leaves is heavy and the robust plant is quite disease tolerant. Unfortunately, the fruits in the photograph don't show the elongated shape of this variety well—it really tends to be more pronounced.

The initial performance of Hungarian Oval in my zone 5 garden was poor. However, it performed very well in the second year and has done well ever since. There's no way to tell if it will need adaptation in the gardens of other growers, but saving seeds and planting them the second year should work as well for you as it did for me.

TYPE: family

ORIGIN: United States

MATURITY: late midseason

COLOR/SHAPE: pink to reddish oval beefsteaks

SIZE/ARRANGEMENT: ranging from about 8 ounces to a pound or more, growing in clusters of two or three

YIELD: usually moderate

PLANT/FOLIAGE: indeterminate habit with heavy cover of regular-leaf foliage

TASTE: assertive, earthy, with wonderful depth

SEEDS: available commercially

Hungarian
Oval

JAUNE FLAMMÉE

W hat sets Jaune Flammée apart from other varieties is the contrast between the orange skin and the reddish interior that is unprecedented in heirloom tomatoes. The appearance is reminiscent of a blood orange. Sometimes, the blossom end also has a bit of a reddish tint. And while the walls of the fruit are quite thick, they're not tough.

This is a small tomato with a very big taste. The flavor literally bursts in your mouth, refreshing and not at all bland. The small orange globes are borne on a sturdy plant that doesn't suffer much from foliage diseases.

Jaune Flammée reminds me of Mini Orange, a variety that is about the same size, but the taste and unique interior coloration of Jaune Flammée make it a far better choice.

TYPE: family

ORIGIN: France

MATURITY: late midseason

COLOR/SHAPE: orange globes, sometimes with a darker reddish blush on the blossom end

SIZE/ARRANGEMENT: bigger than cherries, about 2 or 3 ounces, growing in clusters of about six

YIELD: very high

PLANT/FOLIAGE: indeterminate habit with medium cover of regular-leaf foliage

TASTE: exciting, tangy, with a pleasing kick

SEEDS: available commercially, Jaune Flammée or Flammée

Jaune
Flammée

JAUNE NEGIB

Most tomatoes that mature early in the growing season tend to be less popular for various reasons related to taste or performance. Jaune Negib is one of the few early tomatoes with good taste, visual appeal, and decent production.

Every so often, environmental conditions will alter the expression of genes. In years past, Jaune Negib has been a very oblate tomato with scalloping around the shoulders, which made it visually striking. But this year the shoulders were completely smooth, which for me took away some of its splendor.

The flattened globes of Jaune Negib can vary from a clear yellow to a light golden color, depending on the weather. Its flavor is delicately mild and pleasing.

The foliage cover for this plant is quite sparse, but sunscald is not usually a problem for varieties that mature early. It has, however, proved to be quite susceptible to early blight, which is true for many early varieties. But Jaune Negib will give you good fruit early in the season to tide you over until later-maturing varieties are available.

TYPE: family

ORIGIN: France

MATURITY: early midseason

COLOR/SHAPE: clear yellow to light golden; very oblate, usually with ribbing or scalloping at the shoulders

SIZE/ARRANGEMENT: usually in the 4- to 6-ounce range, growing in clusters of four or five

YIELD: moderate

PLANT/FOLIAGE: indeterminate habit with sparse cover of regular-leaf foliage

TASTE: charming, smooth, on the light side

SEEDS: not available commercially

*Jaune
Negib*

JEFFERSON GIANT

This variety is frequently characterized as heart shaped. The description, however, is questionable because Jefferson Giant doesn't really taper to a point like the other true heart-shaped heirlooms—tomatoes like German Red Strawberry, Anna Russian, and Nicky Crain all narrow down to a distinct point on the blossom end of the fruits. So I describe Jefferson Giant as a fat heart that doesn't taper.

The true appeal of Jefferson Giant is the taste. In fact, the aroma alone is enough to drive the average grower to eat the fruits right off the vine. The flavor is sumptuous and robust, with earthy and sweet undertones and a slight zip. Jefferson Giant is also a wildly juicy tomato. Note the large open spaces (called locules) in the flesh of the cut tomato in the photograph. In general, the greater the number of locules, the juicier the tomato.

The deep pink fruits on this plant are remarkably free of blemishes, and are borne on large plants with spindly, sparse foliage. Despite the thin cover, sunscald has not been a problem, and the foliage has been reasonably tolerant of disease. The fruits mature to about 1 pound each in my zone 5 garden, and have been known to get even larger under ideal growing conditions. Despite its name, Jefferson Giant won't win any massive-tomato contests—this one is for pure eating enjoyment.

TYPE: family

ORIGIN: United States

MATURITY: late

COLOR/SHAPE: deep pink fat hearts or beefsteaks

SIZE/ARRANGEMENT: 1 pound or more, growing in clusters of two or three

YIELD: moderate to high

PLANT/FOLIAGE: indeterminate habit with sparse cover of regular-leaf foliage

TASTE: full, complex, with earthy and sweet tones and a slight bite

SEEDS: available commercially

Jefferson Giant

KELLOGG'S BREAKFAST

There isn't another large orange beefsteak variety that I'd rather grow than Kellogg's Breakfast. The whopping taste of this mighty tomato is truly unequaled, and it's juicy and meaty at the same time. Before I grew this variety, Amana Orange was my orange beefsteak of choice, but Kellogg's Breakfast has proved to be far superior in both taste and performance.

The vibrant deep orange fruits appear on a large plant. Kellogg's Breakfast is a prolific producer of mostly blemish-free tomatoes, although some stitching can be seen at times. The finely dissected foliage is a bit floppy but not sparse, and sunscald has not been a problem. I've never seen blossom end rot on this variety.

TYPE: family

ORIGIN: United States

MATURITY: late midseason

COLOR/SHAPE: vibrant orange beefsteaks

SIZE/ARRANGEMENT: usually 1 pound or more, growing in clusters of two or three

YIELD: high

PLANT/FOLIAGE: indeterminate habit with medium cover of narrow, regular-leaf foliage

TASTE: rich, scrumptious, a blockbuster

SEEDS: available commercially

*Kellogg's
Breakfast*

KIEV

Kiev is a phenomenally juicy and succulent tomato—one bite, and it will be dripping all over you. It has a classic tomato taste: robust, smooth, and not too sweet. Because of its flavor, size, and mouthwatering juiciness, this variety has become a favorite for salsas and other sauces.

Kiev has consistently produced well for me in my zone 5 garden, but the shape has varied from time to time. Within a given plant, fruits can appear as 1-pound elongated plums or almost square-shaped. The plant would be considered semi-determinate—it is less sprawling than most indeterminate tomatoes.

The leaves are very narrow, but the foliage cover is usually excellent. Concentric cracking at the stem end has always been present in Kiev, so it won't win any beauty contests, but that won't affect the glorious taste.

TYPE: family

ORIGIN: Ukraine

MATURITY: midseason

COLOR/SHAPE: elongated red plums

SIZE/ARRANGEMENT: ranging from about 10 ounces to well over a pound, growing in clusters of two or three

YIELD: high

PLANT/FOLIAGE: semi-determinate habit with medium cover of narrow, regular-leaf foliage

TASTE: lovely balanced flavors, not sweet

SEEDS: available commercially

Kiev

LARGE PINK BULGARIAN

The contrast of Large Pink Bulgarian's deep pink fruits against its rich green foliage almost makes you forget that most people grow this tomato because of the superb taste. Like the other Bulgarian varieties, its flavor is big and bold yet also manages to remain complex. And its heavyweight status doesn't stop there—the flesh is firm and dense, and fruits usually weigh in around 1 pound but can reach up to 3 pounds.

Large Pink Bulgarian loads up nicely with gorgeous tomatoes that grow in tight clusters. With the exception of some occasional stitching, this variety's fruits are generally blemish-free. The vines may appear spindly at first, and the foliage cover is not dense, but this doesn't seem to affect the healthy yield. I've never encountered blossom end rot with Large Pink Bulgarian. It has also remained relatively free of foliage diseases.

TYPE: family

ORIGIN: Bulgaria

MATURITY: late midseason

COLOR/SHAPE: dark pink beefsteaks

SIZE/ARRANGEMENT: 12 ounces to over a pound, sometimes up to 3 pounds, growing in clusters of two or three

YIELD: moderate to high

PLANT/FOLIAGE: indeterminate habit with medium cover of regular-leaf foliage

TASTE: sublime, astonishingly full-bodied, on the sweet side

SEEDS: available commercially

*Large Pink
Bulgarian*

LIDA UKRAINIAN

The term "family" heirloom tomato often refers to the large number of varieties that arrived with immigrants who came to America between the mid-1800s and the early 1920s. Although the practice of saving seeds is no longer as common as it once was, some fantastic varieties will occasionally arrive with newly immigrated families. Lida Ukrainian and Sandul Moldovan were brought over recently in this manner.

The fruits of Lida Ukranian are small, globe-shaped, and deep red. The yield is very good, with fruits usually in the 4- to 6-ounce range, growing in clusters of three to five. They are very firm and meaty, and last well on the vine. The taste, which is what attracted me to this variety, is not sweet at all, but reminiscent of the older varieties from the late 1800s in being robust and full-bodied.

The plant is small and somewhat compact for an indeterminate variety, and is best described as semi-determinate. Lida Ukrainian has been remarkably healthy in my garden, with no concentric cracking or foliage disease to speak of.

TYPE: family

ORIGIN: Ukraine

MATURITY: midseason

COLOR/SHAPE: red globes

SIZE/ARRANGEMENT: about 4 to 6 ounces, growing in clusters of three to five

YIELD: high

PLANT/FOLIAGE: semi-determinate habit with heavy cover of regular-leaf foliage

TASTE: excellent, assertive, not sweet

SEEDS: available commercially

*Lida
Ukrainian*

LILLIAN'S YELLOW HEIRLOOM

This variety has not appeared in the catalogs that feature heirloom tomatoes, and with very good reason—it has practically no seeds. In fact, there were several years when I was unable to offer it to fellow Seed Savers Exchange members because of the low seed yields and high demand.

Lillian's Yellow ("Heirloom" is part of the proper name but is often left off) is unique in many ways. It is the only large yellow beefsteak with potato-leaf foliage that ripens to a light, clear yellow instead of turning gold. The creamy consistency of the very meaty flesh also separates it from other varieties. Its taste is deep and complex, with rich, citrusy yet slightly sweet flavors.

The yield for Lillian's Yellow is not high, and the fruits are not always blemish free. Often they have variable shapes, sometimes rough shoulders, and occasionally catfacing when pollination occurs at low temperatures. Because of the potato-leaf foliage, however, this variety has been quite disease tolerant in my garden, and never have I seen blossom end rot. It does mature very late, and would not be a recommended variety for exteme Northern growers. Lillian's Yellow is usually available to Seed Savers Exchange members, but the low seed yield may prevent it from being available commercially for a while.

TYPE: family
ORIGIN: United States
MATURITY: late
COLOR/SHAPE: clear light yellow beefsteaks
SIZE/ARRANGEMENT: usually in the 1-pound-plus range, growing in clusters of two or three

YIELD: moderate
PLANT/FOLIAGE: indeterminate habit with heavy cover of potato-leaf foliage
TASTE: outstanding citrus flavors, sweet and rich
SEEDS: available commercially

*Lillian's Yellow
Heirloom*

MANYEL

Many growers claim that Manyel is absolutely the best-tasting yellow tomato. The somewhat zingy, citruslike flavor is actually so good that you may be tempted to overlook its problems with early blight, which can be controlled. This variety produces at a high level throughout the summer, with flush after flush of fruit. The perfect yellow globes are uniformly blemish free, but do suffer from cracking due to heavy rains (as the photograph attests).

Manyel is somewhat spindly at first, but soon starts growing with vigor. Because of the comparatively sparse foliage cover, there are problems with sunscald late in the season.

This is one of many varieties believed to have originated with Native Americans, but there is no way of authenticating the ancestry of most of them. It's unfortunate, because many "living museums" want to grow these heirloom varieties, but won't if there is no documentation.

TYPE: family

ORIGIN: United States

MATURITY: midseason

COLOR/SHAPE: clear yellow, turning to golden at maturity; usually globular, sometimes oblate

SIZE/ARRANGEMENT: ranging from about 10 ounces to 1 pound, growing in clusters of three to five

YIELD: high

PLANT/FOLIAGE: indeterminate habit with sparse cover of regular-leaf foliage

TASTE: lemony, with a touch of sweetness

SEEDS: available commercially

Manyel

MARIZOL GOLD

Marizol Gold has been among the best gold-red bicolor performers in my zone 5 garden, along with Regina's Yellow and Big Rainbow. The yield is acceptable, the flavor is very good in most years, and the tomatoes usually don't develop the prominent concentric cracking often seen with most of the other red-gold bicolors.

The foliage of Marizol Gold is unusual because it has a distinct blue tinge. The plants bear well, which is not true of some of the larger gold-red bicolors. In most years, the fruits are quite oblate and have pretty ribbing at the shoulders (not present in the photograph). Almost all of the gold-red bicolor types will show splitting in heavy moisture. In the absence of moisture, they often still show concentric cracking that doesn't heal over well and can become infected with bacteria and molds. Marizol Gold does better than most in this regard.

The taste of Marizol Gold can vary. Some summers the soft tomatoes have a very sweet, fruity flavor; in other years, the flavor is mild enough to be considered bland. The visual appeal of these varieties when sliced is outstanding, with reddish orange undertones streaking throughout the flesh.

TYPE: family

ORIGIN: Germany

MATURITY: late midseason

COLOR/SHAPE: gold-red oblate beefsteaks, usually with ribbing at the shoulders

SIZE/ARRANGEMENT: about 1 to 2 pounds, growing in clusters of two or three

YIELD: moderate

PLANT/FOLIAGE: indeterminate habit with medium cover of regular-leaf foliage

TASTE: fruity and sweet in good summers, bland in others

SEEDS: available commercially

Marizol
Gold

MARTINO'S ROMA

The yield of Martino's Roma is absolutely overwhelming. This is a determinate variety (one of the few in my collection) with deep green rugose foliage that grows to about 3 feet tall. It loads up with dark red pear-shaped fruits that make it look like a Christmas tree until the tomatoes reach maturity—then the plant falls over.

Many paste tomatoes are susceptible to early blight, but this variety is quite tolerant. And while most paste types are also very susceptible to blossom end rot, Martino's Roma has not been affected as much as other paste tomatoes I know of.

It is unfortunate that hybridizers don't consider using Martino's Roma or similar varieties like Heidi, Wuhib, or Tadesse as sources for new varieties because their tolerance to blossom end rot is superior to that of the commercial hybrids, which chronically suffer from this condition.

TYPE: family

ORIGIN: Italy

MATURITY: midseason

COLOR/SHAPE: red pears

SIZE/ARRANGEMENT: about 2 ounces, growing in clusters of four to six

YIELD: high

PLANT/FOLIAGE: determinate habit with heavy cover of rugose-leaf foliage

TASTE: pleasant enough but not intense, typical for a paste tomato

SEEDS: available commercially

Martino's Roma

MARY ANN

Mary Ann is an extremely consistent performer, and it can be counted on year after year to produce a healthy bounty of reddish orange beefsteaks. It has been noted that this variety sets fruit better in warmer climates, but I find that it has done quite well in my zone 5 garden. The fruits are generally unblemished and mature late in the midseason.

Mary Ann is a vigorous plant with a heavy dark green foliage cover of regular leaves that contrasts nicely with the tight clusters of fruit. It has shown good tolerance of foliage diseases, and I've seen no blossom end rot. Although indeterminate in habit, it remains relatively compact and doesn't sprawl with long runners, as do most indeterminate varieties.

TYPE: family

ORIGIN: United States

MATURITY: late midseason

COLOR/SHAPE: reddish orange beefsteaks, slightly oblate

SIZE/ARRANGEMENT: usually in the 1-pound range, sometimes larger, growing in clusters of two to four

YIELD: moderate

PLANT/FOLIAGE: indeterminate but relatively compact habit with heavy cover of regular-leaf foliage

TASTE: simply a nice, old-fashioned flavor, not sweet

SEEDS: available commercially

Mary Ann

MATCHLESS

[AUSTIN STRAIN]

This tomato is a worthwhile addition to any heirloom collection because of its gorgeous dark green rugose foliage and classic old-fashioned tomato taste. Many growers use it for canning because the walls of the oblate fruits are very thick.

The Austin strain of Matchless is a small, semi-determinate plant that doesn't need staking. Because of its heavy foliage cover, you may have to look carefully to gather all the maturing reddish orange tomatoes at the bottom of the plant. Rugose-leaf varieties have always been very tolerant of foliage diseases in my garden; the leaves are very thick and probably don't allow for good penetration of the fungal disease spores as they germinate.

Matchless is a representative of an early commercial variety—the Burpee Seed Company introduced it in 1889. The Austin strain of Matchless is different from the strain offered by the USDA under the same name—the USDA strain is less tasty and not as red, and has a somewhat mushy consistency.

TYPE: commercial

ORIGIN: United States

MATURITY: midseason

COLOR/SHAPE: reddish orange; oblate

SIZE/ARRANGEMENT: in the 6- to 8-ounce range, growing in clusters of two to four

YIELD: moderate

PLANT/FOLIAGE: semi-determinate habit with heavy cover of rugose-leaf foliage

TASTE: classic, strong and tomatoey, without pronounced sweetness

SEEDS: not available commercially

Matchless

[Austin Strain]

MATINA

Matina is one of the few good early varieties that perform well and have a taste equivalent in strength and character to that of a beefsteak. The fruits are absolutely perfect—small, globe-shaped, and produced in abundance—and the huge plants continue fruiting well into the summer. Some people report that the first fruits may be mealy, but I haven't experienced that problem. Actually, I think this tomato is almost as good as Stupice, which many consider the standard for an early variety.

Matina is uniformly blemish free and has never shown blossom end rot. The potato-leaf foliage, which is extremely rare on a plant with red fruit, is usually more resistant to fungal and bacterial foliage diseases than most regular-leaf varieties. The foliage grows in heavily, which prevents sunscald.

My best information suggests that Matina is an open-pollinated German commercial variety and not a family-type heirloom. It has been around for about 35 years and is still widely grown in Germany by home gardeners.

TYPE: commercial

ORIGIN: Germany

MATURITY: early

COLOR/SHAPE: red globes

SIZE/ARRANGEMENT: usually 3 to 5 ounces, growing in clusters of five to nine

YIELD: high

PLANT/FOLIAGE: indeterminate habit with heavy cover of potato-leaf foliage

TASTE: excellent, hearty, full-bodied

SEEDS: not available commercially

Matina

MORTGAGE LIFTER

Mortgage Lifter is a large pink-fruited beefsteak that has a good, solid taste—not a knockout, but smooth and mild. It is not a particularly juicy tomato, but is quite firm and keeps well both on and off the vine. The fruits never get huge, usually staying in the 1-pound range, and are usually blemish free. Mortgage Lifter is a big plant with a medium to high yield, depending on the weather.

Many newcomers to heirloom tomatoes are attracted to the name and history of this variety. Its original development was related by Dr. Jeff McCormack of the Southern Exposure Seed Exchange, who taped an interview with M. C. Byles of Logan, West Virginia, the developer of Mortgage Lifter. The history has been liberally used by others in catalog descriptions because the story is so appealing.

M. C. Byles planted four varieties with large fruit: German Johnson, "Beefsteak," an Italian variety, and an English variety. One variety was planted in the middle and the other three varieties surrounded it. Byles took pollen from the outer three varieties and cross-pollinated the blossoms of the center plant. The next year, he planted the best seedling in the middle and surrounded it with three other seedlings. After selecting the best plants each year for six years, he had a stable variety—which he called Mortgage Lifter because he sold plants for $1 each during the 1940s and paid off his $6,000 house mortgage in only six years.

TYPE: family

ORIGIN: United States

MATURITY: late midseason

COLOR/SHAPE: deep pink beefsteaks

SIZE/ARRANGEMENT: to 1 pound and larger, growing in clusters of two or three

YIELD: moderate to high

PLANT/FOLIAGE: indeterminate habit with medium cover of regular-leaf foliage

TASTE: sweet yet rich, very good

SEEDS: available commercially

*Mortgage
Lifter*

MULE TEAM

Mule Team is very similar to Box Car Willie, and comparisons are usually made between the two tomatoes. Both varieties come from the same source, so the similarities are understandable, but there are differences. Mule Team has a high yield of almost perfect, globe-shaped fruits with just a hint of ribbing at the stem end that is not seen in Box Car Willie. The yield and performance of both varieties is comparable to or better than the performance of hybrids.

Mule Team is the perfect tomato for the heirloom skeptic. Not only are the fruits blemish free, but I've never seen blossom end rot or sunscald, and the plants are quite tolerant of foliage diseases, especially in the South. The well-balanced flavor is very pleasing—zippy and sweet at the same time.

TYPE: created

ORIGIN: United States

MATURITY: midseason

COLOR/SHAPE: red globes with slight ribbing at the stem end

SIZE/ARRANGEMENT: usually in the 10- to 12-ounce range, some larger, growing in clusters of three to five

YIELD: high

PLANT/FOLIAGE: indeterminate habit with heavy cover of regular-leaf foliage

TASTE: a nice combination of sweetness and zip

SEEDS: available commercially

Mule Team

NECTARINE

Several tomato varieties are named after fruits such as peaches and nectarines because they very closely resemble their coloration, they have a matte, nonshiny skin, or they're even a bit fuzzy. Unfortunately, Nectarine's similarities to the fruit of its namesake end with appearance. The taste often varies markedly from year to year, from wonderfully sweet to disappointingly bland.

Nectarine closely resembles Peach Blow Sutton but is quite different from Garden Peach, which is the most widely available of these varieties. Among the several strains of Garden Peach, the most common ones have somewhat blocky fruit with coloration that pales when compared to the deep rich reds and yellows of Nectarine.

This is a vigorous plant with a heavy foliage cover of regular leaves. It produces a high yield of blemish-free fruits, and has been free of blossom end rot. Some people may consider it a novelty-type tomato not worth growing for taste, but I have enjoyed some luscious fruits from Nectarine.

TYPE: family

ORIGIN: United States

MATURITY: midseason

COLOR/SHAPE: reddish yellow, slightly oblate globes with green shoulders until fully ripe

SIZE/ARRANGEMENT: mostly in the 4- to 6-ounce range, growing in clusters of three to five

YIELD: high

PLANT/FOLIAGE: indeterminate habit with heavy cover of regular-leaf foliage that shows a touch of hairiness

TASTE: very sweet to bland, depending on the year

SEEDS: available commercially

Nectarine

NICKY CRAIN

This variety deserves distinction because it performs much better than other heart-shaped varieties, which tend to have low yields and variable flavor. The yield for Nicky Crain is moderate when compared to other heirlooms, but downright prolific in the world of heart-shaped varieties. And its taste is also outstanding—rich, but not too sweet.

Nicky Crain produces large, firm, well-formed fruits. Consistency of shape is usually not common to heart-shaped tomatoes, but this one bears nearly perfect fruits throughout the summer. The yield is usually blemish free, and I've never seen any blossom end rot.

Nicky Crain looks spindly with its wispy, droopy foliage, but it grows vigorously. It has narrow, finely dissected leaves that sag. Ironically, this somewhat listless foliage usually means that the fruits to follow will be superb. (Huge, marigoldlike blossoms and potato-leaf foliage also tend to indicate excellent taste in the subsequent fruit.) Because the foliage is sparse, sunscald may be a problem with this variety.

TYPE: family

ORIGIN: unknown

MATURITY: late midseason

COLOR/SHAPE: medium pink hearts

SIZE/ARRANGEMENT: usually in the 1-pound range, many larger, growing in clusters of two or three

YIELD: moderate

PLANT/FOLIAGE: indeterminate habit with sparse cover of finely dissected, regular-leaf foliage

TASTE: superior, complex, not too sweet

SEEDS: available commercially

Nicky Crain

NOIR DE CRIMÉE

A mong the black-type tomatoes available, Black from Tula and Noir de Crimée are the best in terms of taste, productivity, and disease tolerance. Black Krim and Noir de Crimée should be the same tomato (their names are synonymous translations), but after growing both, I discovered they weren't. The fruits of Noir de Crimée turned a much darker color when grown in my zone 5 garden; it was also more productive than Black Krim and the taste was superior. Many people describe the flavor of black-type heirlooms as being slightly salty, but I disagree. What I experience is a rich, dusky, earthy flavor that is slightly sweet.

This medium-size plant consistently produces a high yield. The fruits will often have green shoulders, which contrast nicely with the dark, rich purplish black color. The globe fruits are not perfect in shape, but are slightly oblate, and they can suffer from concentric cracking.

I have never listed Noir de Crimée with the Seed Savers Exchange because many folks have already listed Black Krim. It would be worthwhile to send seeds out for trial, but since the similar variety is already widely available as Black Krim, it would be difficult to persuade people that this strain is superior. The same problem exists with Golden Queen—it is widely available, but the strain I have is superior to the ones listed, and more closely matches the original Livingston description of the tomato.

TYPE: family

ORIGIN: Russia

MATURITY: midseason

COLOR/SHAPE: deep purplish black at maturity, usually with green shoulders; slightly oblate

SIZE/ARRANGEMENT: mostly in the 4- to 6-ounce range, growing in clusters of five to seven

YIELD: high

PLANT/FOLIAGE: indeterminate habit with medium cover of regular-leaf foliage

TASTE: earthy, dusky, slightly sweet

SEEDS: Black Krim is available commercially; Noir de Crimée is not

Noir de Crimée

OLENA UKRAINIAN

Olena Ukrainian is a large pink-fruited beefsteak with a gorgeous canopy of potato-leaf foliage. The overall physical beauty of this variety just can't be overstated—the blemish-free fruits are truly stunning on the vine. I've never observed blossom end rot with this tomato, and it rarely shows any clefts. Sometimes, as with most large beefsteaks, fruits will split after bouts of high moisture.

This is a typical pink beefsteak in that the taste is impressive—sweet yet tangy. The flesh has a nice ratio of juice to meat. The yield is also quite prolific for such a large beefsteak.

This particular variety was involved in a study that tested susceptibility to early blight. In a field that included hybrids—some that were known to be susceptible to early blight and some that showed tolerance—Olena Ukrainian not only thrived, but showed the least damage from early blight when compared to all the other varieties.

The original source of this variety is Olena Warshona from Odessa, Ukraine. I named the tomato after her.

TYPE: family

ORIGIN: Ukraine

MATURITY: late

COLOR/SHAPE: deep pink beefsteaks

SIZE/ARRANGEMENT: in the 1- to 2-pound range, growing in clusters of two or three

YIELD: moderate to high

PLANT/FOLIAGE: indeterminate habit with heavy cover of potato-leaf foliage

TASTE: sweet yet tangy, with great depth, intense

SEEDS: available commercially

Olena Ukrainian

OMAR'S LEBANESE

If you're after huge tomatoes, look no further—Omar's Lebanese is one of the few varieties that can grow as large as 3 or 4 pounds. What's more, the colossal fruits have superb flavor—in taste terms, this tomato is truly worth its weight in gold. The pink beefsteaks are borne in profusion on vigorous plants that have been quite tolerant of foliage diseases.

Although the plant's foliage cover is not heavy, there haven't been problems with sunscald, which is often seen on late-maturing varieties like this one. Concentric cracking can appear (as seen in the photograph) but it heals over nicely and doesn't affect the fruit in any way unless there are heavy rains.

TYPE: family

ORIGIN: Lebanon

MATURITY: late midseason

COLOR/SHAPE: pink beefsteaks

SIZE/ARRANGEMENT: minimum of 1 pound, often as much as 3 or 4 pounds, growing in clusters of two or three

YIELD: high

PLANT/FOLIAGE: indeterminate habit with medium cover of regular-leaf foliage

TASTE: absolutely outstanding, sweet, rich, complex

SEEDS: available commercially

*Omar's
Lebanese*

OPALKA

The uninitiated heirloom grower is usually fascinated by the seemingly unique shape of Opalka. There are, however, many varieties of long red paste tomatoes. Among the ten elongated varieties I've grown, this one is the best. Opalka has been offered in the Seed Savers Exchange brochures for the general public, and the comments of various SSE members in the yearbook are almost uniformly positive.

What distinguishes this variety from others is the taste. Most paste tomatoes—whether they are plums, pears, or the long types—just don't have good taste. Opalka is the exception, and the sweet, refreshing flavor is so good it can be eaten fresh off the vine. The regular-leaf foliage is wispy and droopy, but the big plant is vigorous, and usually has a high yield. Occasionally, the earliest fruits develop blossom end rot, but it disappears quickly.

Although Opalka is excellent for sauce, it's trying for us seed savers because there are practically no seeds. And its dearth of seeds is one of the reasons it has taken so long for this variety to be offered commercially.

TYPE: family

ORIGIN: Poland

MATURITY: midseason

COLOR/SHAPE: red elongated (usually about 4 to 6 inches)

SIZE/ARRANGEMENT: about 6 to 8 ounces, growing in clusters of two to five

YIELD: high

PLANT/FOLIAGE: indeterminate habit with medium cover of regular-leaf foliage

TASTE: excellent, very pleasing, with sweet overtones

SEEDS: available commercially

Opalka

ORANGE STRAWBERRY

This lovely, heart-shaped tomato is always well formed with a sharp tip at the base and a gorgeous deep orange color that just about throbs. The taste is strong and sweet, unlike most orange tomatoes, which tend to be bland. The flesh is quite dry, so those looking for a really juicy tomato might be disappointed.

The leaves are wispy and droopy, yet the plant is still vigorous. Although the yield is not high at all, that shouldn't stop you from growing such an outstanding variety. The fruits of Orange Strawberry are uniformly blemish free.

This variety is not related to German Red Strawberry, but the source of the seeds is the same. A fellow Seed Savers Exchange member sent me the seeds and said that the variety had appeared in her garden from seeds sown from a commercial pack of the tomato Pineapple, which is a large golden-red bicolor.

TYPE: mystery

ORIGIN: United States

MATURITY: late midseason

COLOR/SHAPE: deep orange hearts

SIZE/ARRANGEMENT: mostly in the 8-ounce to 1-pound range, growing singly or in pairs

YIELD: moderate

PLANT/FOLIAGE: indeterminate habit with medium cover of regular-leaf foliage

TASTE: rich and sweet

SEEDS: available commercially, as Orange Strawberry or German Orange Strawberry

Orange
Strawberry

PALE PERFECT PURPLE

Pale Perfect Purple bears perfect globes of a beautiful dusky pink color. It was a selection of a cross between Ozark Pink and Purple Price, which is a black-pink potato-leaf type.

Pale Perfect Purple is soft-fleshed, delicious, and very juicy, having received the best attributes of both parents. Its great richness is imparted by Purple Price and is combined with the sweetness of the Ozark Pink parent. The fruits are always blemish free, and I've never seen blossom end rot on this variety. The foliage is lush and quite tolerant of foliage diseases. The yield is consistently high, and the plant is large but not overwhelming. Very heavy rains that occurred at one point during photography account for the split fruits you see in the picture—normally, that would not happen.

Pale Perfect Purple is listed several ways in the Seed Savers Yearbook: it can also be found under Perfect Purple and Purple Perfect. The reason for the confusion comes from Tad Smith, the hybridizer of the variety, who listed it differently in its first and second years of existence. And the alliteration of the name certainly doesn't bode well for clarifying the matter. I've called it Pale Perfect Purple after one of the original listings.

TYPE: created

ORIGIN: United States

MATURITY: midseason

COLOR/SHAPE: perfect dusky pink globes

SIZE/ARRANGEMENT: mostly in the 6- to 8-ounce range, growing in clusters of four or five

YIELD: high

PLANT/FOLIAGE: indeterminate habit with heavy cover of potato-leaf foliage

TASTE: sweet, rich, exquisite

SEEDS: available commercially, as Pale Perfect Purple, Perfect Purple, or Purple Perfect

*Pale Perfect
Purple*

PEACH BLOW SUTTON

Peach Blow Sutton has a sticky surface not often found in tomatoes. When bearing its ripened fruits, this variety is simply gorgeous to look at. While considered a novelty type, it's worth growing to expand your heirloom experience. The plant is vigorous, with a high fruit yield, and has been quite tolerant of disease. I've observed no blossom end rot, and the fruits have been uniformly blemish free.

My initial reaction to Peach Blow Sutton was not favorable, but I've come to appreciate its unconventional qualities. Varieties such as Peach Blow Sutton, Nectarine, and other matte-surfaced tomatoes named after fruits can, in some summers, have wonderful taste. The flavor is not strong, but it is very sweet in a good year. However, there has not been much consistency of flavor from one summer to the next.

This variety was introduced by Sutton's Seed in England in their 1900 catalog.

TYPE: commercial

ORIGIN: England

MATURITY: midseason

COLOR/SHAPE: orange, red, and yellow blend; peachlike shape

SIZE/ARRANGEMENT: mostly in the 5- to 7-ounce range, growing in clusters of five

YIELD: moderate to high

PLANT/FOLIAGE: indeterminate habit with medium cover of regular-leaf foliage that shows a touch of hairiness

TASTE: in a good year sweet and delicious, in a bad year bland

SEEDS: not available commercially

Peach Blow
Sutton

PINK ICE

Pink Ice is a very firm, solid, deep pink cherry tomato. The "Ice" part of its name remains a mystery, but it could very well have something to do with the firmness of the fruit. The yield is extremely high—as is the case with nearly all cherry tomatoes—with clusters of perfect fruits that stay on the vine in excellent shape for a long time. In this regard, Pink Ice resembles the pink cherry Amish Salad, and is a good bet for market gardeners who need a nonperishable tomato.

Pink Ice is among the three best pink cherry tomatoes that I have grown, along with Amish Salad and Pink Ping Pong. The taste is on the mild side, but still has a pronounced, lingering tomato flavor. The fruits are beautiful oval cherries. This is a huge plant with a heavy cover of regular-leaf foliage.

TYPE: family

ORIGIN: unknown

MATURITY: midseason

COLOR/SHAPE: deep pink oval cherries

SIZE/ARRANGEMENT: 2 to 3 ounces, growing in clusters of five to seven

YIELD: very high

PLANT/FOLIAGE: indeterminate habit with heavy cover of regular-leaf foliage

TASTE: quite good, mild but with a nice tomato taste

SEEDS: not available commercially

Pink Ice

PINK PING PONG

Pink Ping Pong is aptly named—it's about the size of a ping-pong ball and has a soft pink color. The fruits were smaller than normal for the photograph, but this is usually not the case—over my many years of growing this variety, it has usually been one of the larger cherry tomatoes in my garden. Like most cherry tomatoes, the yield is high, the fruits are blemish free, and blossom end rot never rears its ugly head. The taste is very sweet, smooth, and juicy.

Aside from Riesentraube, Dr. Carolyn, Galina's, Green Grape, and Mirabell, I don't grow cherry tomatoes for taste alone. They are fantastic for salads and snacking, and for all the different colors and shapes. This is an excellent variety for the market gardener, since an interesting variety of colors and shapes is appealing to both chefs and the general public.

This variety was in the collection of Andrew Rahart, who lived just north of New York City, and who collected varieties from the ethnic groups in his area. The other excellent variety from Mr. Rahart, Andrew Rahart's Jumbo Red, is also included in this book.

TYPE: family

ORIGIN: United States

MATURITY: midseason

COLOR/SHAPE: light pink cherries

SIZE/ARRANGEMENT: normally 3 to 4 ounces (ping-pong-ball size), growing in clusters of three to five

YIELD: high

PLANT/FOLIAGE: indeterminate habit with heavy cover of regular-leaf foliage

TASTE: delicious, balanced, with pleasant sweetness

SEEDS: available commercially

Pink Ping Pong

PINK SWEET

A tomato's name can have a great influence on its acceptance: without a name, its appeal is somehow lessened in the eyes of the grower. This variety was initially received as "no name," which likely hurt its popularity. At the very least, the name Pink Sweet (given by Craig LeHoullier) accurately describes the color and flavor. The flavor, in fact, is not just sweet, but very rich and intense. The fruits are very soft, and the flesh is quite juicy.

Pink Sweet is a large plant that bears blemish-free light pink globes that are sometimes oblate. The yield and overall vigor are excellent. The plant has a medium foliage cover of regular leaves, and has been susceptible to early blight.

TYPE: family

ORIGIN: United States

MATURITY: late midseason

COLOR/SHAPE: light pink globes, sometimes oblate

SIZE/ARRANGEMENT: usually in the 10-ounce to 1-pound range, growing in clusters of two or three

YIELD: moderate to high

PLANT/FOLIAGE: indeterminate habit with medium cover of regular-leaf foliage

TASTE: very rich, sweet, complex, just wonderful

SEEDS: available commercially

Pink Sweet

PLUM LEMON

From a visual standpoint, Plum Lemon is worth growing for its looks alone—the bright yellow and gold fruits actually shine amid the deep green foliage. This variety is indeed shaped like a lemon, and does even have a slight citrusy flavor to it. The shape qualifies it as a novelty type, but the taste can be quite good. Some people find it bland, but I find the flavor pleasingly mild with that hint of citrus. Of course, flavor components are greatly influenced by environmental conditions and fertilizers—the taste of Plum Lemon is simply variable from year to year.

This is a huge plant with a medium foliage cover of regular leaves that are tolerant of foliage diseases. Plum Lemon's yield is uniformly high every year. The flesh is meaty, more firm than soft, and the fruits are almost always blemish free, with never a trace of blossom end rot.

At least one other lemon-shaped variety is also from Russia, which leads to speculation that the original mutation for this shape occurred in that part of the world. Seed for Plum Lemon was obtained in 1991 by Kent Whealy, cofounder of the Seed Savers Exchange, from an old seedsman in Moscow.

TYPE: family

ORIGIN: Russia

MATURITY: midseason

COLOR/SHAPE: yellow ripening to golden; lemon-shaped

SIZE/ARRANGEMENT: mostly 4 to 5 ounces, growing in clusters of five to seven

YIELD: high

PLANT/FOLIAGE: indeterminate habit with medium cover of regular-leaf foliage

TASTE: surprisingly mild, pleasant, with a hint of citrus

SEEDS: available commercially

Plum Lemon

POLISH C

Polish C is an absolutely wonderful, reliable performer in the garden. It has a robust tomato taste, with just a bit of sweetness and a pleasant bite. The fruit itself has a remarkable balance of juice to flesh, which helps the flavors really linger on the palate. Polish C colors up nicely to a deep pink with brick-red undertones at maturity. Its yield is not outstanding, but it is steady.

The fruits are usually unblemished except for a tendency toward concentric cracking. Some splitting (as seen in the photograph) can occur due to heavy rains. The foliage cover for this variety is noticeably light compared with that of most other potato-leaf varieties, but sunscald is not a problem. Polish C has been tolerant of foliage diseases, and has never shown blossom end rot.

Potato-leaf foliage can spontaneously mutate to a regular-leaf form, and Polish C did this in my garden. Seed stock of both leaf forms results in identical fruits.

TYPE: family

ORIGIN: Poland

MATURITY: late midseason

COLOR/SHAPE: deep pink beefsteaks

SIZE/ARRANGEMENT: mostly in the 1-pound range, growing in clusters of two or three

YIELD: moderate

PLANT/FOLIAGE: indeterminate habit with medium cover of potato-leaf foliage

TASTE: very full, complex, with a nice edge

SEEDS: available commercially

Polish C

RASP LARGE RED

There are fewer quality red heirloom types than there are pink varieties. Rasp Large Red is special because it is a relatively new red heirloom with wonderful taste and solid performance. The plant is large but more compact than most indeterminate varieties, and it has a sparse to medium foliage cover of small, narrow leaves.

The taste of Rasp Large Red is authoritative, not mild, and appeals to those who like the strong taste of old-fashioned tomatoes. It has a complex balance of tart and sweet flavors. The fruits are deep red globes, and they contrast nicely with the dark green foliage. Most fruits are in the 10- to 12-ounce range, and the yield is steady throughout the growing season.

This variety was introduced to Seed Savers Exchange in 1984 by T. Rasp of Cheektowaga, New York.

TYPE: family

ORIGIN: United States

MATURITY: late

COLOR/SHAPE: red globes, sometimes oblate

SIZE/ARRANGEMENT: mostly in the 10- to 12-ounce range, sometimes to 1 pound, growing in clusters of two or three

YIELD: moderate

PLANT/FOLIAGE: indeterminate but compact habit with sparse to medium cover of narrow, regular-leaf foliage

TASTE: high-flavored, with nicely balanced tartness and sweetness

SEEDS: available commercially

Rasp Large Red

REDFIELD BEAUTY

Redfield Beauty is a commercial open-pollinated heirloom that is amazingly similar to Eva Purple Ball. The two varieties are discernable because Redfield Beauty is a lighter color and the plant is less substantial. However, the two are alike in size (about 6 to 8 ounces) and in the number of fruits per cluster (three to five), and they also share the tendency to drop tomatoes from the vine when ripe. The most striking similarity is the fact that Redfield Beauty has the same faint surface mottling of white as Eva Purple Ball. The fruits of both taste alike—sweet and rich—although to me Eva Purple Ball has slightly better flavor.

Redfield Beauty produces perfect pink globes with abandon. The foliage cover is adequate, and the regular leaves are narrow and small. The plant grows with an open habit that allows the fruits to be prominently displayed.

Redfield Beauty is listed as a synonym for Beauty, a variety introduced by the Livingston Seed Company in 1886, and is said to be a selection made by another seed company. I've grown Beauty from USDA seeds, and that strain doesn't have the characteristics mentioned above that are common to both Eva Purple Ball and Redfield Beauty.

TYPE: commercial

ORIGIN: United States

MATURITY: midseason

COLOR/SHAPE: perfect pink globes with a white surface mottling

SIZE/ARRANGEMENT: about 6 to 8 ounces, growing in clusters of three to five

YIELD: high

PLANT/FOLIAGE: indeterminate habit with medium cover of regular-leaf foliage

TASTE: sweet, pleasant, soft on the palate

SEEDS: available commercially

Redfield Beauty

RED PEAR

Everyone loves this cute little red cherry tomato. The elongated pear-shaped fruits are wildly popular because their looks make them appealing for salads, as a garnish, or for snacking out of hand. Luckily, their beauty makes up for the so-so taste, which can be described as very mild, but which is a step above bland. I, for one, would never be without them.

Red Pear yields in abundance, like most cherry tomatoes. The plant is a huge sprawling thing just loaded with clusters of fruit, only slightly less prolific than Yellow Pear. It is much more tolerant of early blight than its yellow cousin, and I've never seen any blemishes, blossom end rot, or other kind of problem with this variety.

The red and yellow small pear varieties probably predate 1800 by many years.

TYPE: family

ORIGIN: unknown

MATURITY: midseason

COLOR/SHAPE: small red pears

SIZE/ARRANGEMENT: about 1 ounce, growing in clusters of seven to nine

YIELD: high

PLANT/FOLIAGE: indeterminate habit with medium cover of regular-leaf foliage

TASTE: mild, but not bland

SEEDS: available commercially

Red Pear

RED PENNA

Red Penna is an outstanding tomato that deserves recognition for its wonderful taste and steady performance in the garden. It bears large red beefsteaks with a very strong, old-fashioned tomato flavor that is best described as full-bodied, with a hint of tartness. The flesh is dense yet juicy, and Red Penna is an excellent candidate for munching right in the garden. One thick slice also makes a terrific tomato sandwich.

Red Penna is a vigorous grower, with a heavy cover of regular-leaves that is very tolerant of foliage diseases. This is an indeterminate plant, but not a sprawler. The fruits seldom show any blemishes, catfacing, or blossom end rot. The shoulders of the tomatoes may be a bit rough and indented, but these problems are simply cosmetic and won't affect the taste.

TYPE: family

ORIGIN: United States

MATURITY: late midseason

COLOR/SHAPE: red beefsteaks

SIZE/ARRANGEMENT: mostly in the 1- to 2-pound range, growing in clusters of two or three

YIELD: moderate to high

PLANT/FOLIAGE: indeterminate habit with heavy cover of regular-leaf foliage

TASTE: superb, robust and tomatoey, not sweet

SEEDS: available commercially

Red Penna

REGINA'S YELLOW

When at its peak, you can't beat the sweet, luscious flavors of Regina's Yellow. Most gold-red bicolor types are visually beautiful—on both the exterior and the interior—but the taste can be highly variable. The same variety that has a sweet, fruity flavor one season may be totally bland the next. When the taste is right, however, the flavors of Regina's Yellow are reminiscent of a fresh fruit salad. The most consistent bicolor varieties for me (along with Regina's Yellow) have been Marizol Gold, Big Rainbow, and Pineapple.

Regina's Yellow yields beautiful, large, blemish-free beefsteaks. The flesh is soft and perishable, as with all bicolors. This variety is one of my favorite gold-red heirlooms because it matures well before the first frost in my zone 5 garden, and has shown comparatively little concentric cracking.

Regina's Yellow didn't color up as vividly as some other bicolors during this particular season. Notice that the cut tomato in the photograph does not show the vivid interior marbling of red that usually occurs when the fruits are perfectly ripe.

TYPE: family

ORIGIN: United States

MATURITY: late midseason

COLOR/SHAPE: gold-red beefsteaks

SIZE/ARRANGEMENT: mostly in the 1- to 2-pound range, growing in clusters of two or three

YIELD: moderate

PLANT/FOLIAGE: indeterminate habit with medium cover of regular-leaf foliage

TASTE: sweet and fruity in a good summer, bland in others

SEEDS: available commercially

Regina's
Yellow

REIF RED HEART

Reif Red Heart is an outstanding red heart-shaped heirloom that more than makes up for its lackluster fruit production with fantastic taste. The taste is a scrumptious blend of rich and zingy flavors with sweet undertones that linger from the first bite to the last. The overpowering aroma alone, however, is capable of winning you over. The flesh is quite heavy and dense, and the fruits color up to a typical tomato red.

The vines on this variety sprawl and are somewhat spindly, but it's a vigorous plant. Actually, I was surprised to find this was an Italian family heirloom because I've seldom seen this type of spindly growth and droopy foliage from areas outside the Slavic countries and Germany. The foliage cover is often sparse, and sunscald may be a problem, but the plant generally produces uniform, blemish-free, great-tasting fruits.

This variety comes from J. Reif of Pennsylvania, who received seeds from an elderly Italian gentleman.

TYPE: family

ORIGIN: Italy

MATURITY: late midseason

COLOR/SHAPE: red hearts

SIZE/ARRANGEMENT: as large as 1 pound, growing in clusters of two or three

YIELD: moderate

PLANT/FOLIAGE: indeterminate habit with sparse to medium cover of regular-leaf foliage

TASTE: delectable, very rich, with a nice blend of sweetness and zest

SEEDS: available commercially, as Reif Red Heart or Reif Italian Heart

*Reif Red
Heart*

RIESENTRAUBE

Most gardeners don't have the space or time to experiment widely with different varieties, but if there is one tomato that absolutely must be grown by heirloom aficionados, Riesentraube is it. The stalks alone create 200 to 300 blossoms that can be picked for a floral display. A mature cluster has 20 to 40 elongated, pointed oval fruits.

Riesentraube means "giant bunch of grapes" or "large grape" in German, which accurately describes the fruit clusters. The plant is vigorous, with a good foliage cover, and the fruits don't show blemishes or splitting after rains. Riesentraube evokes a broad spectrum of flavor components that you just don't expect in a cherry tomato. The taste is very full, like that of a beefsteak.

Plants grown from saved seed don't always give me the huge clusters typical of this variety—in a recent growing season, only one of three plants had the expected large clusters.

Riesentraube has long been grown in Europe, especially in Germany, and was available in Philadelphia in the mid-1800s. A friend even made wine from it—as was done in the past—and it had a delicious, pale sherry taste.

TYPE: family

ORIGIN: Germany

MATURITY: midseason

COLOR/SHAPE: red elongated cherries with a pointed tip

SIZE/ARRANGEMENT: 1 ounce, developing from a blossom stalk with literally hundreds of flowers into fruit clusters of 20 to 40

YIELD: high

PLANT/FOLIAGE: indeterminate habit with heavy cover of regular-leaf foliage

TASTE: amazingly intense tomato taste, not sweet, just superb

SEEDS: available commercially

Riesentraube

RUSSIAN #117

Russian #117 is a superlative heirloom. In addition to its outstanding taste, this variety is unique because of its curious form—it bears a high percentage of double flat heart-shaped fruits. (The configuration of double flat hearts is best explained by visualizing a normal heart tomato cut in half and folded out.) The fruits of Russian #117 are so dense that you could imagine them going through a concrete floor. And the flavor is gargantuan, with intense sweet bursts and a healthy amount of juice to go along with the hearty flesh.

Russian #117 is a sprawler with the characteristic wispy, droopy foliage common to many heart-shaped tomatoes. What distinguishes it from other red hearts is the excellent productivity, extremely large size of the fruits (often up to 2 pounds), and continued yield until frost. The fruits are blemish free.

Seed Savers Exchange members who list this variety have praised it very highly. The #117 is the SSE accession number, and it does help to distinguish this outstanding tomato from all the other varieties called "Russian." This variety is excellent for pasta sauce because it's so meaty, but I prefer to eat it fresh off the vine.

TYPE: family

ORIGIN: Russia

MATURITY: late midseason

COLOR/SHAPE: flat red hearts, many of them double

SIZE/ARRANGEMENT: mostly in the 1- to 2-pound range, growing in clusters of two or three

YIELD: moderate to high

PLANT/FOLIAGE: indeterminate habit with sparse to medium cover of regular-leaf foliage

TASTE: very robust but balanced, sweet yet zippy

SEEDS: available commercially

Russian #117

SANDUL MOLDOVAN

Sandul Moldovan has a powerful, almost sugary nectar that is treasured by those in search of the telltale sweetness found in many heirloom tomatoes. The flesh is dense, and even close to creamy.

The fruits are deep pink beefsteaks, usually with slight ribbing at the shoulders. Normally they are blemish free, but cracking due to heavy rains can occur (and it did on the fruits in the photograph). Many varieties show concentric cracking when very heavy moisture levels are present during the growing season.

Despite the wispy, droopy foliage, Sandul Moldovan is a vigorous plant and produces a very high yield of lovely fruits. I've not seen blossom end rot or sunscald, although the leaves have been somewhat susceptible to foliage diseases.

The seeds for this variety came from the Sandul family, who recently arrived in the United States from Moldova. Like so many other immigrants, they brought their treasured family plant heirlooms with them.

TYPE: family

ORIGIN: Moldova

MATURITY: midseason

COLOR/SHAPE: deep pink beefsteaks, with slight ribbing at the shoulders

SIZE/ARRANGEMENT: mostly in the 12-ounce to 1-pound range, growing in clusters of three to five

YIELD: high

PLANT/FOLIAGE: indeterminate habit with medium cover of regular-leaf foliage

TASTE: predominantly sweet but not overpowering

SEEDS: available commercially

Sandul
Moldovan

SANTA CLARA CANNER

Santa Clara Canner is believed to be the variety responsible for starting the tomato canning industry in California. The walls are extremely thick but yet the skin is not tough. In fact, the taste is realized more through the juice because of this surprising thickness of the walls. The flavor is smooth and light-bodied, sweet but not intense. All these qualities make this tomato perfect for canning. Another variety, known as Diener, is a selection of Santa Clara Canner that is more red in color.

The fruits can grow so close together that sometimes they become deformed. And the bottom of the plants must be carefully checked for developing ripe tomatoes because the regular-leaf foliage cover is so heavy that it can hide the fruits. Visually, this heavy cover of deep green leaves is a beautiful counterpoint to the reddish orange beefsteaks. Most of the fruits are beautifully formed and blemish free—Santa Clara Canner will seldom exhibit anything more than a bit of stitching.

This variety may need adaptation in your garden. The first year of growing it resulted in only three fruits, but saved seeds planted the next year gave rise to a very nice harvest and things have remained that way ever since.

TYPE: family

ORIGIN: Italy

MATURITY: late

COLOR/SHAPE: reddish orange beefsteaks

SIZE/ARRANGEMENT: about 1 to 2 pounds, growing tightly packed in clusters of three to five

YIELD: moderate to high

PLANT/FOLIAGE: indeterminate habit with heavy cover of regular-leaf foliage

TASTE: very sweet, smooth

SEEDS: available commercially

Santa Clara Canner

SOLDACKI

Soldacki has a taste intensity that is tangy and strong on the palate, yet with a pronounced sweetness, and the complexity of flavors remains constant from start to finish. There is also a nice balance of flesh to juice.

Soldacki doesn't keep well on the vine, and will develop concentric cracking the longer it waits to be picked. It has a distinct tendency to crack at the stem end (as seen in the photograph). However, many people are willing to put up with this habit because the taste and yield are so superior. This is a huge plant with a high yield of dark pink beefsteak fruits. Aside from the tendency to crack, the fruits are usually blemish free, and I've never seen blossom end rot. The vigorous potato-leaf foliage is quite tolerant of diseases.

Soldacki was passed down through an extended family that came from Krakow, Poland, to Cleveland, Ohio, around 1900.

TYPE: family

ORIGIN: Poland

MATURITY: late midseason

COLOR/SHAPE: dark pink beefsteaks

SIZE/ARRANGEMENT: mostly in the 1-pound range, with some larger, growing in clusters of two or three

YIELD: high

PLANT/FOLIAGE: indeterminate habit with heavy cover of potato-leaf foliage

TASTE: luscious, intense, with a good ratio of sweetness to tartness

SEEDS: available commercially

Soldacki

SOPHIE'S CHOICE

S ophie's Choice has a number of qualities that make it unique and worth growing. It's a small determinate plant with red, oblate fruits that ripen very early and are remarkable in size (6 to 8 ounces) for such an early tomato. Its taste is also uncharacteristically strong for an early-season variety, and is equal to that of later-maturing tomatoes. The flavor is full bodied and smooth—it's not subtle but it doesn't scream at you, either. I find it very agreeable. The fruits are very firm, almost hard.

The determinate plant is very compact and short, often not exceeding 18 inches in height. The foliage cover of regular leaves is very heavy, and is quite tolerant of early fungal diseases. In the photograph you'll notice that the leaves are curled. This often happens on any variety with a heavy fruit burden in combination with certain environmental conditions. The fruit production is high for such a small plant, and the heavy fruits often make the plant tip over, so support might be advised.

This variety can be finicky with regard to its growing conditions. It seems to like wet feet (damp soil) during early growth. If dry conditions prevail, it doesn't produce fruits and you end up with stunted plants. Most years it produces reliably, however, and is one of the only early tomatoes I recommend, along with Stupice and Matina.

TYPE: family
ORIGIN: Canada
MATURITY: early
COLOR/SHAPE: red; oblate
SIZE/ARRANGEMENT: mostly 6 to 8 ounces, growing tightly packed in clusters of two or three

YIELD: high
PLANT/FOLIAGE: determinate habit with heavy cover of regular-leaf foliage
TASTE: refreshing, youthful but smooth, a bit sweet
SEEDS: available commercially

Sophie's Choice

STUPICE

Stupice has long been the gold standard of early-maturing heirloom tomatoes. The plant is indeterminate but compact. The 3- to 4-ounce fruits, produced in clusters, appear early and continue producing for a long time. The tomatoes are unblemished, but the photograph shows splitting that resulted from very heavy rains. Potato-leaved foliage helps this variety resist early foliage diseases.

Stupice has a good flavor that is sweet, tangy, and altogether reminiscent of a beefsteak. The color is an intense red, and the juicy, globe-shaped fruits are borne in abundance.

Pronounced stoo-PEECH-ka, this tomato was hybridized, selected, and genetically stabilized in Czechoslovakia. For years its origin has been mistakenly attributed to M. Sodomka. He introduced this variety (along with many other selections) outside Czechoslovakia, but was not the original hybridizer.

TYPE: created

ORIGIN: Czechoslovakia

MATURITY: early to early midseason

COLOR/SHAPE: deep red globes

SIZE/ARRANGEMENT: about 3 to 4 ounces, growing in clusters of three to five

YIELD: high

PLANT/FOLIAGE: indeterminate but compact habit with medium cover of potato-leaf foliage

TASTE: full-flavored, with a nice balance, very enjoyable

SEEDS: available commercially

Stupice

SUTTON

Newcomers to heirloom tomatoes are often drawn to white and other unconventional colors. Obviously, the fruits from white heirloom varieties are not completely white—tomatoes that develop under the foliage will be pale ivory, and those exposed to the sun during maturation can be pale yellow to light yellow. Most white tomatoes have a pink blush at the blossom end that doesn't extend into the flesh. The flesh tends to remain lighter than the outer skin color.

The taste of most white varieties is so bland that they're not worth growing. But folks who love a mild sweet tomato need look no further—Sutton has a sweet, engaging, fruity taste and a creamy flesh. The fruits are 6- to 8-ounce flattened globes, produced heavily throughout the summer. The medium cover of regular leaves has shown good tolerance of foliage diseases.

Some people call this variety Sutton's White, but the proper name is simply Sutton.

TYPE: mystery

ORIGIN: unknown

MATURITY: midseason

COLOR/SHAPE: pale ivory to light yellow, sometimes with a pink blush at the blossom end; oblate

SIZE/ARRANGEMENT: mostly 6 to 8 ounces, growing in clusters of three to five

YIELD: high

PLANT/FOLIAGE: indeterminate habit with medium cover of regular-leaf foliage

TASTE: mild, fruity, sweet but refreshing

SEEDS: not available commercially

Sutton

TANGELLA

The vibrant orange globes of Tangella are known and grown for their intense flavor. For such a small tomato, the taste is quite tangy and has a real zest to it. This is a very firm tomato that doesn't split (unlike its sibling Tigerella). The plant is large, and the dark green foliage contrasts nicely with the deep orange coloring of the fruits.

Tangella's fruits, borne in abundance, are larger than those of a cherry tomato but they're still small. Although the foliage cover of regular leaves is not extensive, I've never seen any sunscald. All the fruits are blemish free, and the plant has been been quite tolerant of foliage diseases.

Tangella is one of three varieties that were selected for and genetically stabilized to an open-pollinated form at the Glasshouse Crops Research Institute in England. The other two varieties were Craigella and Tigerella (which is the original Mr. Stripey).

TYPE: created

ORIGIN: England

MATURITY: midseason

COLOR/SHAPE: orange globes

SIZE/ARRANGEMENT: about 2 to 3 ounces, growing in clusters of seven to nine

YIELD: high

PLANT/FOLIAGE: indeterminate habit with medium cover of regular-leaf foliage

TASTE: robust, distinctively tart, not sweet

SEEDS: not available commercially

Tangella

TIFFEN MENNONITE

Seeds for this variety have been commercially available for twenty years—a long time by heirloom tomato standards. As a result, Tiffen Mennonite has many devotees who cherish and grow it every season for its good production and sweet, mild taste. The fruits are big, heavy, dense things with some ribbing at the shoulders; occasionally, they are malformed and exhibit clefts.

Tiffen Mennonite grows into a huge plant, and the yield of deep pink beefsteaks is quite heavy. The medium cover of potato leaves is tolerant of foliage diseases, and I've never seen any blossom end rot with this variety.

TYPE: family

ORIGIN: United States

MATURITY: late midseason

COLOR/SHAPE: deep pink beefsteaks

SIZE/ARRANGEMENT: mostly in the 1-pound-plus range, growing in clusters of two or three

YIELD: moderate to high

PLANT/FOLIAGE: indeterminate habit with medium cover of potato-leaf foliage

TASTE: pleasant, light, smooth and sweet

SEEDS: available commercially

Tiffen
Mennonite

UKRAINIAN HEART

[O'NEILL STRAIN]

There are several varieties named Ukrainian Heart, so it's important to identify them by their origin with a strain designation. Along with the two Ukrainian Heart varieties listed here (the TNMUJ strain follows this entry), Anna Russian and Nicky Crain are the best pink heart-shaped heirlooms in terms of taste and performance. The O'Neill strain of Ukrainian Heart is notable for its yield, which is average compared to other tomatoes but absolutely outstanding for a heart-shaped variety.

Ukrainian Heart will exhibit differences in fruit shape on the same plant, from longer, skinny hearts to fatter, more blunt ones. The taste is mild, sweet, and not as rich as the other three pink heart-shaped varieties mentioned above. The fruit is soft fleshed, which is typical of the pink heart varieties. The typical wispy, droopy regular-leaf foliage is sparse, and combined with the open habit of the plant, subjects the fruit to possible sunscald late in the season.

TYPE: family

ORIGIN: Ukraine

MATURITY: midseason

COLOR/SHAPE: medium pink hearts

SIZE/ARRANGEMENT: usually in the 1-pound range, growing in clusters of two or three

YIELD: moderate

PLANT/FOLIAGE: indeterminate habit with sparse cover of finely dissected, regular-leaf foliage

TASTE: sweet, mild, refined

SEEDS: not available commercially

Ukrainian Heart

[O'Neill Strain]

UKRAINIAN HEART

[TNMUJ STRAIN]

This particular pink heart has seniority in my garden, which means that it's a longtime favorite. The taste of this strain is much richer than that of the O'Neill strain. It is also quite sweet, but is much more robust and exciting. The foliage cover is more substantial than that of most heart-shaped varieties, which may be an advantage in areas where sunscald is a problem late in the season. The yield is excellent for a heart-shaped tomato.

Except for a bit of concentric cracking, this strain of Ukrainian Heart is uniformly blemish free and beautiful. Its only drawback seems to be its tendency to cross easily with others. Exerted stigmas—which stick way out beyond the anthers—may make this variety prone to insect pollination rather than normal self-pollination, but this has not been proved. As a precautionary measure for plants like this, never plant all your seeds of a given variety. Always hold back some in case an accidental cross or some other calamity occurs.

TNMUJ is the Seed Savers Exchange identification code for the seed source, Jerry Murphy of Tennessee (TN).

TYPE: family

ORIGIN: Ukraine

MATURITY: late midseason

COLOR/SHAPE: medium pink hearts

SIZE/ARRANGEMENT: about 1 to 2 pounds, growing in clusters of two or three

YIELD: moderate to high

PLANT/FOLIAGE: indeterminate habit with medium cover of finely dissected, regular-leaf foliage

TASTE: rich, luscious, quite sweet

SEEDS: not available commercially

Ukrainian Heart

[TNMUJ Strain]

WHITE QUEEN

White Queen is as close to a pure white tomato as you'll find. It is also the best-tasting variety of its color, being both fruity and sweet, and not bland like almost all the other white tomatoes. The blossom end of many white tomatoes often shows a pink blush (seen at the top left in the photograph). Many times the blush will be even more intense than here, but the color doesn't extend to the interior.

The yield of White Queen is absolutely outstanding, and the plant keeps producing fruits with abandon throughout the summer. The habit is open, so tomatoes that appear later in the season will color up more and not remain as "white" as those that appear early in the growing season. White Queen's fruits are quite oblate, and ribbing occurs around the stem end. The flesh is wonderfully creamy.

White Queen is especially popular with those who love to make white pasta sauce.

TYPE: commercial

ORIGIN: United States

MATURITY: midseason

COLOR/SHAPE: white to pale ivory to light yellow; oblate, with ribbing at the shoulders

SIZE/ARRANGEMENT: about 6 to 8 ounces, growing in clusters of three to five

YIELD: high

PLANT/FOLIAGE: indeterminate habit with medium to heavy cover of regular-leaf foliage

TASTE: sweet, fruity, a palate refresher

SEEDS: available commercially

White Queen

WINS ALL

Wins All is a model of consistency. Season after season, this variety produces a trove of mouthwatering, blemish-free fruits. The taste is sweet yet zippy, and memorable from the first bite to the last. The firm and juicy tomatoes keep very well on the vine, and the plant almost never suffers from foliage diseases or blossom end rot.

Several people have noted the modest fruit production, but plants grown from seed obtained from several sources have consistently provided moderate to high yields for me. When saving seed, it's important to select fruits that represent all size and shape variations within a variety. In this way, genetic diversity within the variety is maintained, and this could help overcome inconsistencies in yield or taste.

Winsall (one word) is the name most people associate with this tomato. It was actually an improvement made by the Henderson Seed Company in the 1920s on Ponderosa, an old pink beefsteak type. Originally assigned a number for identification, this variety was labeled Wins All as a result of a naming contest.

TYPE: commercial
ORIGIN: United States
MATURITY: late midseason
COLOR/SHAPE: medium pink beefsteaks
SIZE/ARRANGEMENT: usually 1 pound or more, growing in clusters of two or three

YIELD: moderate to high
PLANT/FOLIAGE: indeterminate habit with heavy cover of regular-leaf foliage
TASTE: complex, intense, sweet yet tangy
SEEDS: available commercially, as Wins All or Winsall

Wins All

WUHIB

Wuhib has a truly unique habit. It is a determinate variety that spreads out horizontally into an immense bush about 18 inches high and often 2 feet across. The taste is somewhat lightweight—mild and slightly sweet to start with, finishing with a certain smoothness. The small red plum fruits are borne in profusion, and will last on the vine for what seems like an eternity.

This variety is particular vigorous when compared to other paste types. Unlike most paste tomatoes, Wuhib has shown remarkably little blossom end rot; it has also shown little susceptibility to foliage diseases, which is quite rare for paste types. In terms of overall performance for paste tomatoes, Wuhib is on a par with Heidi, Opalka, and Martino's Roma.

Tadesse Wuhib, a former student of mine, brought back these seeds from a farmer's market in Addis Ababa, Ethiopia. Their origin likely explains their ability to withstand high heat.

TYPE: family

ORIGIN: Ethiopia

MATURITY: late midseason

COLOR/SHAPE: small red plums

SIZE/ARRANGEMENT: about 4 ounces, growing in clusters of five to seven

YIELD: high

PLANT/FOLIAGE: determinate habit with heavy cover of regular-leaf foliage

TASTE: very subtle, somewhat sweet

SEEDS: not available commercially

Wuhib

YELLOW PEAR

Yellow Pear was historically used for tomato preserves, but more recently has become the rage in salads and as a garnish (cut lengthwise) at high-end restaurants. And baskets of Yellow Pear, alone or with its sibling Red Pear, are a big hit with growers at farmers' markets. Their appeal is that they're awfully cute. Most people find the taste to be very mild and occasionally sweet—I grow them mostly for snacking.

The plant is large and sprawling, absolutely loading up with cluster after cluster of shiny yellow fruits. The foliage of Yellow Pear is quite susceptible to early blight, unlike that of Red Pear. As with most cherry tomatoes, blossom end rot has never been a problem.

Yellow Pear has shown remarkable staying power. It has been clearly documented as a pre-1800 variety, and remains wildly popular today.

TYPE: family

ORIGIN: unknown

MATURITY: midseason

COLOR/SHAPE: small yellow to golden pears

SIZE/ARRANGEMENT: about 1½ to 2 ounces, growing in clusters of seven to nine

YIELD: very high

PLANT/FOLIAGE: indeterminate habit with medium cover of regular-leaf foliage

TASTE: very mild, sweet

SEEDS: available commercially

Yellow Pear

ZOGOLA

Every year I grow Zogola, it outproduces almost every tomato in my garden. The luscious beefsteaks grow so close together in clusters that this can sometimes lead to a few deformed tomatoes. The deep red fruits are usually prominently ribbed at the stem end, and may have small belly buttons. The taste of Zogola is equal to its huge fruit size: noble, strong, and wonderfully full bodied.

The cut tomato in the photograph nicely displays the ratio of flesh to seed locules, which are the seed compartments. This indicates Zogola's degree of meatiness, which is substantial. Neither heavy rains nor drought seem to bother this variety. One year the fruits were puffy and a bit hollow inside, but that was likely an aberration.

The heavy cover of regular leaves is very tolerant of foliage diseases, and I've never seen any blossom end rot with Zogola.

TYPE: family

ORIGIN: Poland

MATURITY: late midseason

COLOR/SHAPE: deep red beefsteaks, with prominent ribbing at the shoulders

SIZE/ARRANGEMENT: in the 2- to 3-pound range, growing tightly packed in clusters of three to five

YIELD: high

PLANT/FOLIAGE: indeterminate habit with heavy cover of regular-leaf foliage

TASTE: full-bodied, rich and tangy, just superb

SEEDS: available commercially

Zogola

Appendix A

COMMERCIAL SOURCES *for* SEEDS AND BOOKS

Following is a list of companies with strong catalog descriptions, service, and available seed product. Tomato Growers Supply Co. and Chuck Wyatt sell the largest number of varieties that are featured in this book.. The other companies are good sources also; no one place lists all the varieties I've described.

TOMATO GROWERS SUPPLY CO.
P.O. Box 2237
Fort Myers, FL 33902
1-888-478-7333
www.tomatogrowers.com

CHARLES A. (CHUCK) WYATT
5421 Princess Dr.
Rosedale, MD 21237
(410) 687-8665
www.heirloomtomatoes.net

SOUTHERN EXPOSURE SEED EXCHANGE
P.O. Box 170
Earlysville, VA
(804) 973-4703
www.southernexposure.com

SEED SAVERS EXCHANGE
3076 North Winn Rd.
Decorah, IA 52101
(319) 382-5990

SANDHILL PRESERVATION
1878 230th St.
Calamus, IA 52729
(319) 246-2299

HEIRLOOM SEEDS
P.O. Box 245
West Elizabeth, PA
(412) 384-0852
www.heirloomseeds.com

BURPEE HEIRLOOMS W. ATLEE BURPEE AND CO.
300 Park Avenue
Warminster, PA 18077
1-800-888-1447
www.burpee.com

SHEPHERD'S GARDEN SEEDS
30 Irene St.
Torrington, CT 06790-6658
(860) 482-3638
www.shepherdseeds.com

PINETREE GARDEN SEEDS
P.O. Box 300
New Gloucester, ME 04260
(207) 926-3400
www.superseeds.com

JOHNNY'S SELECTED SEEDS
2258 Foss Hill Rd.
Albion, ME 04910
(207) 437-4301
www.johnnyseeds.com

COOKS GARDEN
P.O. Box 535
Londonderry, VT 05148
(800) 457-9705
www.cooksgarden.com

RECOMMENDED BOOKS

BREED YOUR OWN VEGETABLE VARIETIES: POPBEANS, PURPLE PEAS, AND OTHER INNOVATIONS FROM THE BACKYARD GARDEN, by Carol Deppe, Little Brown and Co., 1993, Boston, London, Paris.

LIVINGSTON AND THE TOMATO, by A.W. Livingston, A. W. Livingston's Sons, 1893, Columbus, OH. (Republished in 1998 by Ohio State University Press, Columbus, Ohio.)

SEED TO SEED, by Suzanne Ashworth, Seed Savers Exchange, 1991, Decorah, IA.

THE TOMATO IN AMERICA: EARLY HISTORY, CULTURE AND COOKERY, by Andrew F. Smith, University of South Carolina Press, 1994.

PHOTOGRAPHY CREDITS

PHOTO EDITOR: Alexandra Truitt; **PHOTO RESEARCH:** Jerry Marshall

Title Page © Michael Howes/Garden Picture Library; vii & 10 © David Cavagnaro; 7 © David Cavagnaro; 13 © Saxon

Holt; 20-21 © David Cavagnaro; 26 © David Cavagnaro; All other photography by Frank Iannotti

Appendix B

SEED SOURCES *for* INDIVIDUAL VARIETIES

The further an heirloom tomato gets from its original source, the greater the chances for changes in the variety due to minor mutations and possibly some cross-pollination. Some varieties appear to have changed little over the years; others have changed considerably. The original source designation can have several connotations. It can mean that the variety originated with that person or the person's family; it can refer to the person who first introduced the variety to SSE, or to the person who hybridized and/or selected it to an OP form; it can also mean the person who was the first to make the variety generally available to others. *Please note that (**OS**) refers to original source and (**MS**) refers to the seed source for the tomatoes pictured in this book.*

AKER'S WEST VIRGINIA: Carl Aker (OS). Craig LeHoullier via Carl Aker (MS).

AMISH PASTE: Unknown (OS). Purchased commercially (MS).

AMISH SALAD: Unknown (OS). John Adams, IL, via local Amish (MS).

ANDREW RAHART'S JUMBO RED: Unknown (OS). Andrew Rahart via his son John (MS).

ANNA RUSSIAN: B. Hellenius, OR, via a Russian immigrant who shared seeds with her grandfather (OS). Craig LeHouiller via B. Hellenius (MS).

AUNT GINNY'S PURPLE: SSE member Rick Burkhart, Indianapolis, IN (OS). Bill Minkey via Rick Burkhart (MS).

AUNT RUBY'S GERMAN GREEN: Ruby Arnold, Greenville, TN (OS). Bill Minkey via Ruby Arnold (MS).

BASINGA: Unknown (OS). Joe Bratka, NJ (MS).

BIG RAINBOW: Dorothy Bieswenger, MN (OS, MS).

BRANDYWINE, OTV: Craig LeHoullier (OS). Cross-pollination took place in LeHouiller's garden, and was genetically purified by me.

BRANDYWINE, PINK [SUDDUTH STRAIN]: Unknown (OS). The Brandywine name refers to a river in PA and hints at possible Amish origin. Craig LeHoullier (MS).

BRANDYWINE, RED: Unknown (OS). Tom Hauch of Heirloom Seeds shared them with Steve Miller of the Landis Museum, who contacted the original SSE source and determined that the variety was named for the Brandywine River in PA, was Amish, and was available by about 1885.

BRANDYWINE, YELLOW [PLATFOOT STRAIN]: Unknown (OS). Barbara Lund, OH, introduced it to SSE via Charlie Knoy, IN. Gary Platfoot of OH (MS).

BREAK O' DAY: Commercial pre-1940 variety (OS). An anonymous SSE member (MS).

BRIANNA: Unknown (OS). Joe Bratka, NJ (MS).

BULGARIAN #7: Unknown (OS). Andrew Smith via his son, who spent time in Bulgaria (MS).

BULGARIAN TRIUMPH: Unknown (OS). Dennis Sherwood, Kenosha, IL (MS).

CHEROKEE CHOCOLATE: Craig LeHoullier (OS, MS). The skin epidermis mutation from Cherokee Purple occurred in his garden.

CHEROKEE PURPLE: Cherokee Nation (OS) as claimed by J.D. Green, TN. Craig LeHoullier via J.D. Green (MS).

CHRIS UKRAINIAN: Krzysztos Szymanski, an employee from the College of Saint Rose (OS, MS).

CRNKOVIC YUGOSLAVIAN: Yasha Crnkovic (OS, MS), from the Vojvod region of Yugoslavia.

CUOSTRALÉE: Unknown (OS). Norbert Parreira, Hellimer, France (MS).

DEBBIE: Unknown (OS). Anonymous SSE member (MS).

DR. CAROLYN: Carolyn Male (OS, MS), named by Steve Draper. A selection from Galina's, a yellow cherry tomato from Siberia.

DR. LYLE: Unknown (OS). George Korbel, WV (MS).

DR. NEAL: Unknown (OS). Bill Ellis, PA, and Will Weaver, PA (MS).

DR. WYCHE'S YELLOW: Dr. Wyche (OS). Craig LeHoullier (MS).

DRUZBA: Unknown (OS). Norbert Parreira, Hellimer, France (MS). The USDA collection also carries this variety. Seeds from both sources were identical.

EARL OF EDGECOMBE: The 7th Earl of Edgecombe (OS). Ulrike Paradine, England (MS).

EVA PURPLE BALL: Joe Bratka, NJ, via his grandparents from the Black Forest area of Germany in the late 1800s (OS, MS).

GERMAID RED: Unknown (OS). Don Podolia, WV (MS).

GERMAN HEAD: Unknown (OS). Gleckler's Seed Co. (now defunct), Metamora, OH (MS).

GERMAN RED STRAWBERRY: Marjorie Morris, IN (OS, MS), whose family brought the seeds from Germany.

GOGOSHA: Tanya Gogosha, Cohoes, NY (OS, MS), a student of mine from the Tarnipal region of Ukraine.

GOLD BALL, LIVINGSTON'S: Livingston Seed Company (OS). Introduced commercially in 1892. USDA (MS).

GOLDEN QUEEN [USDA STRAIN]: Alexander Livingston of the Livingston Seed Co. made selections from yellow tomato bought from a farmer (OS) at a county fair. Livingston introduced it commercially as Golden Queen in 1882. USDA (MS).

GREEN (DOROTHY'S GREEN): Dorothy Beiswenger, MN (OS). Craig LeHoullier (MS).

GREEN GAGE: Unknown (OS). Probably a pre-1800 variety. USDA (MS).

GREEN GRAPE: Tom Wagner (OS, MS).

GREEN ZEBRA: Tom Wagner (OS, MS).

GROSSE COTELÉE: Unknown (OS). Norbert Parreira, Hellimer, France (MS).

HEIDI: Heidi Iyok, Cameroon, Africa (OS, MS).

HERMAN'S YELLOW: Unknown (OS). Joe Bratka, NJ (MS).

HUGH'S: Madison County, IN (OS). Craig LeHoullier (MS).

HUNGARIAN OVAL: Possibly Karen Gulick, MD (OS). Jerry Murphy, TN (MS).

JAUNE FLAMMÉE: Unknown (OS). Norbert Parreira, Hellimer, France (MS)

JAUNE NEGIB: Unknown (OS). Norbert Parreira, Hellimer, France (MS).

JEFFERSON GIANT: Unknown (OS). Purchased commercially (MS).

KELLOGG'S BREAKFAST: Darrell Kellogg, MI (OS). Bill Minkey via Darrell Kellogg (MS).

KIEV: Unknown (OS). Al Lefkowitz, NY, via a Ukrainian neighbor (MS).

LARGE PINK BULGARIAN: Unkown (OS). John Adams, IL (MS).

LIDA UKRAINIAN: Andy Durbak, Albany, NY (OS, MS).

LILLIAN'S YELLOW HEIRLOOM: Lillian Bruce, TN (OS). Craig LeHoullier (MS).

MANYEL: Unknown (OS), but thought to be of Native American origin. Joe Bratka, NJ (MS).

MARIZOL GOLD: Joe Bratka, NJ (OS). From the Black Forest region of Germany in the late 1800s by his grandparents. A town called Maria's Zell is thought to be responsible for the name.

MARTINO'S ROMA: Unknown (OS). Maureen Conway, NY (MS).

MARY ANN: Unknown (OS). Joe Bratka, NJ (MS).

MATCHLESS [AUSTIN STRAIN]: Unknown (OS). Introduced commercially by Burpee in 1889. Matchless seeds are available through the USDA. Dale Austin (MS).

MATINA: Unknown (OS). Probably an OP commercial variety. Bill Malin via a German Seed Bank (MS).

MORTGAGE LIFTER: M.C. Byles, Logan, WV (OS). Commercially purchased (MS).

MULE TEAM: Joe Bratka, NJ (OS, MS).

NECTARINE: Unknown (OS). USDA (MS).

NICKY CRAIN: Unknown (OS). Carl Aker, PA, via Craig LeHoullier (MS).

NOIR DE CRIMÉE: Unknown (OS), although all black types originated in the former USSR. Norbert Parreira, Hellimer, France (MS).

OLENA UKRAINIAN: Olena Warshona (OS). John Bartkowski (MS).

OMAR'S LEBANESE: Omar Saab (OS, MS).

OPALKA: Opalka family (OS). Opalka family via Carl Swidorski, NY (MS).

ORANGE STRAWBERRY: Unknown (OS). Marjorie Morris, IN (MS), a renegade seed from a package of Pineapple (bicolor) seeds.

PALE PERFECT PURPLE: Tad Smith (OS, MS), hybridized, selected, and purified from the parents Purple Price and Ozark Pink.

PEACH BLOW SUTTON: Unknown (OS). Kees Sahin, Holland, made contact with Tom Sharples of Sutton Seeds and confirmed that Peach Blow Sutton was introduced commercially in the 1900 Sutton Seed Catalog. USDA (MS).

PINK ICE: Unknown (OS). Joe Bratka, NJ (MS).

PINK PING PONG: Unknown (OS). John Rahart via his father, Andrew (MS).

PINK SWEET: Unknown (OS). An anonymous SSE member via Craig LeHouiller, who named the variety (MS).

PLUM LEMON: Unknown (OS). Seeds were obtained in Moscow by Kent Whealy of SSE. Purchased commercially (MS).

POLISH C: Unknown (OS). Robert Richardson, NY (MS).

RASP LARGE RED: T. Rasp, Cheektowaga, NY (OS). T. Rasp via Craig LeHoullier (MS).

REDFIELD BEAUTY: Unknown (OS). Redfield Beauty is listed as a synonym for Beauty, which was introduced by the Livingston Seed Co. of Ohio in 1886. USDA (MS).

RED PEAR: Unknown (OS). Probably a pre-1800 variety. Purchased commercially (MS).

RED PENNA: Unknown (OS). Robert Richardson, NY (MS).

REGINA'S YELLOW: Regina Yanici, OH (OS). Robert Richardson, NY (MS).

REIF RED HEART: J. Reif, PA (OS). J. Reif via Craig LeHoullier (MS).

RIESENTRAUBE: Unknown (OS). A very old European variety that has been documented by Will Weaver as being grown in PA in the mid 1800s. Craig LeIouiller via Curtis Choplin, who received seeds from the German Seed Bank (MS).

RUSSIAN #117: Unknown (OS). Marie Kodoma (MS).

SANDUL MOLDOVAN: The Sandul family (OS). Andy Durbak (MS).

SANTA CLARA CANNER: Unknown (OS). USDA (MS).

SOLDACKI: Soldacki family (OS). Carmen Artino, whose family brought them from Krakow, Poland, to the US in 1900 (MS).

SOPHIE'S CHOICE: Unknown (OS). Barry Comden, CA (MS).

STUPICE: A Czechoslovakian hybridizer whose seeds were distributed by M. Sodomka (OS). Purchased commercially (MS).

SUTTON: Unknown (OS). Craig LeHoullier (MS).

TANGELLA: Glasshouse Crops Research Institute, England (OS). John Tinsley, England (MS).

TIFFEN MENNONITE: Unknown (OS). Faxon Stinnett, OK (MS).

UKRAINIAN HEART [O'NEILL STRAIN]: T. O'Neill, PA (OS). T. O'Neill via Craig LeHoullier (MS).

UKRAINIAN HEART [TNMUJ STRAIN]: Unknown (OS). Jerry Murphy, TN (MS).

WHITE QUEEN: Unknown (OS). USDA (MS). The USDA cites a commercial listing in the Earl May Seed Catalog of 1941.

WINS ALL: Unknown (OS). Faxon Stinnett, OK (MS). Wins All was an improvement on the pink beefsteak Ponderosa made by the Henderson Seed Co. in the 1920s.

WUHIB: Unknown (OS). Tadesse Wuhib (MS), from a market in Addis Ababa, Ethiopia.

YELLOW PEAR: Unknown (OS). Probably a pre-1800 variety. Purchased commercially (MS).

ZOGOLA: Unknown (OS). Joe Bratka, NJ (MS).